How to M

A Cc

Atatürk's Büyük Nutuk and Augustine's City Of God

How to Mend a Broken World:

A Comparative Study of
Atatürk's *Büyük Nutuk* and Augustine's *City Of God*

Published by
The Village Wordsmith
1822 Wheats Valley Road
Bedford, VA 24523 USA.

All rights reserved. No part of this publication may be reproduced, stored in a retrieval system, or transmitted in any form or by any means, electronic, mechanical, recording or otherwise, without the prior written permission of the author.

Manufactured in the United States of America

ISBN 9781761025542

Table of Contents

Acknowledgments

I salute the faculty and my peers at Regent University, who imparted an ideal of scholarship and the scholarly community. Dr. Keeler's classes were always a pleasure, and his sponsorship of this dissertation has been invaluable. Yes, one can acquire a world-class education online, one that blends academic and personal challenges.

Many gracious people made this work possible. First, of course, were my parents, Thomas D. and Helen Smedley, who catechized me in the Catholic faith, imparting a sense of the reality of the transcendent order. I also appreciate the influence of many peers over the years. The folks at Fish House in Roanoke, Virginia, shared the 1970 "Jesus movement" with me, a "Narnia year" that left behind a residue of amazing memories, and riddles that fueled decades of reflection and research. Paul Sherman and Philip Casterline, Pentecostal preachers, imparted an enduring sense of the majesty and holiness of God. Keith Johnson, a disciple of Francis Shaefer, put the Christian faith to work in a Florida street mission, and trained his staff to do the same in their dealings with others. Rich Edwards, PhD, modeled Christian scholarship, productivity, and the imperative need for Christians to use their minds for the glory of God. Jimmie Hollandsworth, pastor of Grace Covenant Church, opened my eyes to the warmth of the Reformed faith. The elect of God are continuously astonished at the goodness of God towards people as unworthy as themselves.

Several Calvinist writers and scholars taught me to appreciate the Reformed perspective. These include Rousas John Rushdoony, the Armenian Calvinist, a man of towering intellect and productivity and his prolific son-in-law Gary

North. The optimism that characterized these scholars transformed my family, vocation, and orientation towards life.

Mentors in the craft of writing include Ron Singleton, PR Director of Ferrum College, who taught me how to engage the reader's attention and bring it in for a landing. Al Anway, a man of great kindness, integrity and precision, gave me the opportunity to break into the profession of technical writing. Paul Hayden brought me in on my first big contract, expected more of me than I thought possible, and guided my interactions with subject matter experts.

My wife since 1978, Vicky K. Smedley, saw in me the man I wanted to be, and helped me to become that man. I appreciate our children who stepped on board for this journey: Greg, who is pursuing a programming career; Dori, who married a programmer, and is a fellow graduate student; and Beth and Laura, who have had less of me these last few years, because of the demands of graduate school.

And, of course, I cannot forget my Turkish friends. Nur and Özgür helped me acquire a basic reading knowledge of their fascinating language, and opened the doors to an exotic, courtly, and hospitable culture. Süleyman and Serap confirmed my positive impression of Turks and Turkish. I fondly recall Hasan and Melahat, the parents who came to Durham, NC in a last effort to save their son's life; Ceren, their daughter, who found the medical facility they used; and Eren, the son of heroes, or, if legend is true, of wolves. Five of his 13 brief years were spent fighting cancer. He faced his last battle nobly, and left a legacy of valor.

Finally, I thank the God who has given me life, wonderful things to do with it, and wonderful people to enjoy it with. At a challenging moment in his academic career, I shared a favorite phrase with Haluk, a language tutor and fellow doctoral student:

Çünkü Tanrı bize korkaklık ruhu değil, güç, sevgi, ve özdenetim ruhu vermiştir.

Because / God / to us / fearful / spirit / not, / power, / love, / and / self-mastery / a spirit / He has given.

I hope that all who read and enjoy this dissertation, Christian and Muslim, American and Turk, will also rejoice in the invisible arms that support us through demanding projects, and demanding times.

How to Mend a Broken World

Overview

Permit me to introduce this book

Umberto Eco's novel *The Name of the Rose* begins with a tedious hundred pages of painstaking detail. As he later explained, those who wished to enter, heart and mind, into the late medieval world of his fictional characters, should expect to do their penance first.

Chapter 1 lays the groundwork for my dissertation by defining the problem I attempt to analyze. Ages end. The end of a given culture appears, to those in the midst of the trauma, to be the end of the world. Most people go inert, hunker down, and wait to see what will happen next. Many panic, and embrace bizarre extremes of thought and behavior. From time to time, however, a remarkable leader emerges to lead the way to a more sustainable social reality. Assuming that some principles are universally valid, hard-wired into the human psyche, I suggest that people from a variety of backgrounds can use these same tools of thought. If a fifth-century African Christian and a 20th century secular Turk can both look at a crumbling empire, say "You know, we can do better than this," and then go on to change the lives of millions, maybe they have something to teach us.

For a number of reasons, the present American empire is not sustainable. But the end of our world is not the same thing as the end of the world. If we can rethink and retool our own lives, we will be prepared to help our neighbors do the same.

Chapter 2 starts by examining the various tools of conviviality that make community possible. It also, indirectly, describes the secular religion that defines life for the vast majority of people who were born in the last few hundred years. No matter where we go to church on Sunday, the same kinds of bureaucrats manage our lives for us the other six days of the week. The same kinds of schools and newspapers seek to integrate us into the same kind of national identity, one rooted in language, culture, and folklore rather than faith in a transcendent God. This is the modern version of "the world" that John warned us about, the systematic structure of thought and action, which asserts that God can safely be ignored. This "civil religion" is indeed a religion, even though it has no explicit deity. The implicit deity of any social order is the source of its laws and the highest level of civil government that it pledges allegiance to. In contemporary America, the Supreme Court claims to be The Ultimate Lawmaker. And most Americans humbly concur. As the clever palindrome puts it, "Do nine men interpret? Nine men, I nod."

Chapter 3 is where the rubber meets the road, and we see how the life work of two world menders could, indeed, be compared in terms of a theological construct. It's also a fascinating glimpse into exciting moments in world history, when things could have turned out very differently than they did, had it not been for wise leaders and inspiring leadership.

Chapter 4 uses quantitative (statistical) techniques to support the comparisons discussed in Chapter 3. In our day, statistics is the sacred liturgical language that provides credibility in the universe of discourse. A message said with numbers becomes more believable, especially if it is counter-intuitive.[1] Since this chapter is also written with a prose style that was trained in a public-relations office, it is fun to read. You can watch science

---

[1] In 1992, I used statistical analysis on matched samples of children in public schools and home schools to demonstrate that the home school children were significantly ahead of their peers in terms of social maturity. My name still turns up on page 1 of google searches more than 20 years later.

(well, *social* science, anyways!) in process, and perhaps acquire a few "tricks of the trade" to use in your own scholarly work.

Chapter 5 first offers a generic set of conclusions, phrased with care to avoid offending either Muslims or the scientific community. Unless leaders do these five things, sound these five notes, their work will have minimal effect. In this release, I add an autobiographical *apologia pro vita sua,* and discuss my own pilgrimage through several worldviews.

Permit me to introduce myself

I was baptized and raised in the Roman Catholic Church, but lured away from the faith at the age of 10 by "science," which, of course, included Darwinism. Genesis and Darwin could not both be true, as I saw then and believe as firmly today. So, given the amazing achievements of modern technology, I reluctantly cast my vote for "science."

Yet, despite all the marvels it placed at our fingertips, technology could not satisfy the primary human need for a relationship with our Creator. The "New Age" movement, with its gospel of a personal relationship with an evolving deity, a god seen as a joint-venture subset of human experience, offered some solace. But attempting to pretend to believe things that you know are not really true is a recipe for lunacy. People who struggle with autistic spectrum disorders find the search for "inner truth" especially damaging. Suppose you spiral into your navel, and can't find your way back to reality, to sanity?

Classmates at Roanoke College and several books, including *Mere Christianity* and *The Cost of Discipleship,* brought the Protestant perspective to my attention. After one last attempt run away from life (on a bicycle), I got with the program in Bristol TN in June 1970. A "Narnia year" began, an epic season displaced from normal time, as thousands of us found ourselves in the middle of a special moment when the miraculous became routine.

Ten years later, the defective elements of this movement had bared their ugly fangs. Many of us lacked a sound perspective on such things as time, work, sexuality and substance abuse. Apocalyptic hysteria led too many to drop out of school, eschew long-range commitments, and launch into a life as "full-time ministers" who hitchhiked around "living by faith." When Jesus did not come down to earth in 1975, we had to. The Seventh Day Adventists speak of their "great disappointment." I know something of how they felt. Chagrin and disillusion backstopped my theological musings. A return to the basics gave me reasons to forge ahead, complete an interrupted college education, marry an amazing woman, and launch into the world of real-world work. But I still wondered. Questioned. Searched.

Then, a friend from the old days dropped back into my life. He gave me a stack of books that blended the sulfur, charcoal, and saltpeter of several orthodox Christian doctrines into an explosive new mix. The authors of those books suggested that people of faith should apply their faith to all of life, not just the internal, mystical, "religious" dimension of life. We are called to make an observable difference in our worlds now, with the expectation that the compounding effect of myriad small acts will ultimately transform everything.

Academic milestones

After ten years of intense self-education, I took my new convictions and insights out for their first test-drive in the world of academia. As the masterpiece of my MS in Corporate and Professional Communication, I applied statistical tools to an exciting sociological issue. My thesis, *Social Maturity of Home School Children: A Communications Approach* objectively tackled the objection commonly heard to home schooling: will the children raised by their parents be adequately "socialized?" My findings, first published in 1992, are still cited.

Like the *ronin* who disappear for a while, I then immersed myself in a technical writing career. I still toyed with a notion to explore more rigorously some day: Atatürk and Augustine both redefined their broken worlds. As we face fearsome fault lines in the American culture, what can we learn from these two men? In 2005, several new beginnings emerged. I began studying Turkish with graduate students met through the Duke Language Partners Program. I gained a better understanding of the way my own mind worked, and learned why I found certain basic skills so problematic, and others so easy. And, I embarked upon the Regent University doctoral program, knowing, from Day One, the focus, aims, and purpose of the dissertation I'd eventually write. Two men offered hope to worlds that were falling apart. One was a Christian, the other wasn't. What did they both do right? What can we learn from them?

Personae Dramatis

Augustine, a 5th-century African bishop, and Atatürk, a 20th-century Turkish nationalist, both addressed the end of an empire by crafting a successful new vision of social order. Augustine's *City of God* (City) defined medieval Europe. Atatürk's *Six Day Speech* (Nutuk) transformed the Turks from the managers of a sprawling Islamic empire into the citizens of a compact, modern republic. To earn my doctorate, I used both qualitative and quantitative techniques to highlight the thematic elements that City and Nutuk share. Since both books achieved a similar real-world result, I assumed they had things in common.

Matthew Fontaine Murray, the land-bound founder of oceanography, explained his passion thus: "The Word of God says there are paths in the sea, *and I intend to find them.*" He collected ships' logs, studied them, and mapped out the ocean currents of the world, the paths in the sea.

With Murray's attitude, expecting to find a specific set of answers to a specific question, I used Meredith Klein's (1963) five-point treaty model as a guide to qualitative research. This "rhetorical criticism" served as a grid to map the common themes these documents shared. Yes, Nutuk and City both addressed all five points with convincing arguments.

Then, I used open-source text analysis software to support the position that these two documents belong to the same genre – useful users manuals for world remakers. A little XML, a little SQL, an idea of what I was looking for, and the numbers emerged to support the original intuition that yes, indeed, there were common elements. **The sea of history had its paths, and they could be found**.

Like Augustine, like Atatürk, we face times of uncertainty. "A mistake in the foundation will chase you all the way to the chimney top," said Bob Jones, homebuilder and mentor. You can incorporate fallacies into the foundation of your social order – but sooner or later, they catch up with you.

As Rome imploded, the gods that held that civic order together lost their power over the imaginations of the people. Athanasius reports that the pagan oracles so many relied upon for guidance fell silent. The primary deity of the Roman world, Rome itself, as incarnated in the "genius of Caesar," became more sworn at than sworn by. Rome no longer provided protection, but pillaged its working citizens to placate urban mobs with *panem et circusum* – bread and circuses. Taxes skyrocketed, and citizens of independent means often went over to the barbarians in order to escape the exactions of the Roman tax farmers. The Roman roads, Roman navies, and Roman courts had provided a zone of stability for the centuries it took for the Christian message to establish its influence over the known world. Now, the termite-ridden scaffolding began its slow-motion collapse. Seen from the inside, the world was coming to an end. Civilization was falling before the relentless migrations that erupted from the steppes of central Asia, and toppled other tribes before them. As Rome contracted, an occasional Welsh officer in Caesar's legions stayed behind, and maintained a Camelot of civil order for a brief but memorable holding action.

But was all lost? With the wisdom of hindsight, we note how monastic orders converted the barbarian tribes of Europe. Christian abbots worked with Jewish merchants to found the great cities of Western Europe at convenient crossroads and fords, the geographical centers of commerce. The monks would build a monastery and begin teaching their neighbors. The merchants organized fairs. After a few hundred years, small cities could invest several generations to erect great cathedrals for the glory of God. Monastery schools became universities. A common culture, a common faith, and a common scholarly language, transformed the "others," the uncouth barbarian enemies of civilization, into Christendom.

Speaking of invaders from central Asia – the Magyars moved into the plains of present-day Hungary, kept their native language, but traded in their pagan gods for Christianity. These people from the East became defenders of the West.

As Yeats opined after the self-destruction of post-Christian Europe,

> Things fall apart; the centre cannot hold;
> Mere anarchy is loosed upon the world,

The blood-dimmed tide is loosed, and everywhere
The ceremony of innocence is drowned;
The best lack all conviction, while the worst
Are full of passionate intensity.

As often happens during times of uncertainty, people of faith circle the wagons and focus their attention on ever-shrinking zones of relevance. The snake oil peddlers are eager to hawk their usual nostrums – mysticism, apocalyptic hysteria, misdirected frantic projects. Yet, ages have ended before, and the world went on. What do our times require of us? What does our God require of us? These are the questions that R. J. Rushdoony, the writer of those books that redirected my life, asked. And began to answer. My humble desire is to suggest, with Dr. Rushdoony, that these are great times to be alive, the future will be different from the present, and it can be far better.

Chapter 1: Problem and Purpose

Much of my professional life has been spent as a technical writer, immersed in the blue-collar branch of the communications business. For several reasons, this career provided excellent preparation for the task at hand of investigating several world-changing documents.

The technical writer who embarks upon a doctoral dissertation brings the driving curiosities of his discipline to bear on the matter at hand. We ask such questions as: What makes things work? What is the best way to do something? How can we explain, in the most succinct way possible, the best or easiest way to get from Point A to Point B? As the academic truism so accurately states, the plural of anecdote is not data. However, unless the singular of data becomes anecdote, the data is singularly pointless, and has nothing to say. Meaningful information has a story to tell, a narrative to further, and fresh insights to enrich our understanding of the matters at hand.

Technical writing requires the practitioner to be a permanent student, always learning new ways to package information. He deals every day with new technologies that need to be explained, and new publishing tools that need to be used to explain the technologies. For us, technology is the equivalent of the Japanese artist's bamboo – both a subject of discourse, and a medium of discourse. This fascination with technology shapes Chapter 4, which relies upon several sophisticated, but accessible, software tools for content analysis.

Professional writers are always reading. Technical writers, too, are bibliophiles who collect and cherish models of excellent how-to communication. For example, to plant a garden, see *The Self-Sufficient Gardener* by John Seymour. To launch a small business, see Don Lancaster's *The Incredible Secret Money Machine*. To build a home, peruse Ken Kern's *The Owner-Built*

Home. To rebuild a shattered culture, why not examine Augustine's *City of God*, and Kemal Atatürk's *Six Day Speech* as though they were technical manuals for world-changers? Karl Marx wrote, "The philosophers have only interpreted the world, the point is to change it" (as cited in *Stanford Encyclopedia of Philosophy*, 2010). If we would change our worlds, we would do well to examine the writings of those who actually did just that. There is no need to re-invent some wheels. We can see further, and achieve more, by standing on the shoulders of giants.

The sphinx demands of us in our day the same question she threw in the faces of other cultures at points of decision amid decline, chaos, and need for change (May, 1969, p. 165). It is the challenge posed to 5th-century Romans, 20th-century Ottomans, Weimar-republic Germans, and Czarist Russians. It is the question that formed the title of an essay by Tolstoy, the question cried out to the heavens by dwarf cameraman Billy Kwan in the movie *The Year of Living Dangerously*: "What then must we do?" (Weir, 1982). Or, as an American scholar who became an Alpine guru to a generation of footloose seekers inquired in the title to one of his books, *How shall we then live?* (Shaeffer, 1976). In the search for some answers to that question, we will examine an overlooked masterpiece by a 20th-century Turkish nationalist, and compare it to the more enduring literary landmark written by a 5th-century African Christian who, like Kemal Atatürk, lived through the decline and fall of a mighty empire, and defined the successor civilization.

What To Do When Ages End?

People get frightened when their social order loses cohesion and credibility. "I am so glad that you are here to tell us about God," Natasha, the charming middle-aged English teacher told the visiting missionary tourist (personal communication, 1992). The motor of the town yacht purred quietly in the background as they enjoyed the glorious Dneiper River, on a cruise sponsored by the town of Slavutich. The northerly latitude tempered the June sunshine on that radiant day in 1992. The city fathers had rolled out the red carpet, hoping to forge cultural and economic connections to these eager visitors from the United States. Slavutich, a city of 20,000 souls, was laid out on a grandiose scheme around a central square, with marble facade over brickwork. Less than four years since the city was launched, the veneer was already coming off the dry fountain in the square. The town's largest building, a Communist Party headquarters, was still under construction, even though the city fathers had no idea what to do with it.

None of the grass was mowed, and people did not walk on it. When American ears heard the word катастрофа in a Russian sentence, the speaker was discussing the event that gave birth to this city, sounded the death knell of the Soviet Empire, and raised the question of radioactive grass clippings – the Chernobyl disaster.

A sense of a profound tragedy hung over Slavutich. In the town museum's room of remembrance, perpetual votive candles burned before somber black and white photographs of young people, engineers in their twenties and thirties, who knowingly went to their deaths trying to contain the disaster. A Russian inscription on the wall is a tribute to the enduring work of those who had died. The last sentence can be roughly translated "If not me, then who?"

The collapse of Communism was a psychological Chernobyl. On the Dnieper River cruise, the English teacher spoke of how she wanted her children to have something worthy to believe in. "We had been told that Ukrainians, Russians, and

Byelorussians were all brothers, working together to build a new world," Natasha explained. "Then, with *glasnost* and *perestroika*, we found out the historical truth." People were not fighting to get into their socialist workers' paradise, but out. The brotherhood between Russians and Ukrainians resembled that of Cain and Abel. (personal communication, 1992)

With their moral order discredited, how can people live? What shall they live for? "I would sometimes hold a pen out at arm's length, and drop it, just to see if the law of gravity still held," reminisced an American who lived for several years in the social chaos of post-soviet Ukraine (Jackson, 2005).

Ancient literature portrayed social collapse as a cosmic catastrophe, with the heavenly bodies going astray (Isaiah 13:9-10, 34:4; Amos 8:9; Ezek. 32:7-8; Matt. 24:29-31). Umberto Eco's novel *The Name of the Rose* (1983) and Huizinga's popular history *The Waning of the Middle Ages* (1954) poignantly document the bewilderment experienced by medieval people living during times of seismic societal tremors. Apocalyptic movements flare up when a tribe becomes sufficiently hopeless. The "ghost dancing" mania of 1890 promised the restoration of the *status quo ante* to obedient, dancing Sioux (Brown, 1981, pp. 406-412). Another recent scholar, Douglas Frank, described the cultural shock of the American fundamentalist Protestants who lost their way towards the end of the nineteenth century. Many of these frightened people of faith assumed that the end of their world, of their familiar social milieu, could only mean the end of the world. "Prophecy teaching" flourished as an anodyne to a present sense of impotence. Soon, yes very soon, the wistful consumers of this pulp literature genre were assured, the world would be turned right side up again, with our side in the driver's seat (Frank, 1986, pp. 60-102).

An Armenian Calvinist mused on events at *The End of an Age* and concluded:

> The end of an age is always a time of turmoil, war, economic catastrophe, cynicism, lawlessness, and distress. But it is also an era of heightened challenge and creativity, and of intense vitality. And because of the intensification of issues, and their world-wide scope, never has an era faced a more demanding and exciting crisis. (Rushdoony, 1980, p. 113)

An age can gradually fade away. A given population quits replenishing itself, and lets its birthrate fall below replacement levels. Other ages fail suddenly in a viole nt *Götterdämmerung*, or cataclysmic event, as societal restraints collapse and the most ruthless elements seize command. The streets run red as the tumbrels (and heads) roll, crystalline shop windows are smashed, and the Red Guard roams and denounces. This can happen almost overnight. As a Marxist Jesuit suggested:

> Some fortuitous coincidence will render publicly obvious the structural contradictions between stated purposes and effective results in our major institutions. People will suddenly find obvious what is now evident to only a few . . . Like other widely shared insights, this one will have the potential of turning public imagination inside out. Large institutions can quite suddenly lose their respectability, their legitimacy, and their reputation for serving the public good. It happened to the Roman Church in the Reformation, to royalty in the Revolution. The unthinkable became obvious overnight: that people could and would behead their rulers. (Illich, 1973, p. 111)

Anxious times, troublesome times, sometimes call forth greatness, and inspire extraordinary, gifted thinkers. At rare moments in history, an exceptional public figure gathers flotsam from the wreckage swirling in the maelstrom around him, and crafts from the debris a new ark, a new vessel for the identity and aspirations of his people. Millions of lives are changed.

Such times also inspire an outpouring of escapist literature. Fantasies about alternate realities may be well written, but rarely affect the course of history. As composer Jan Sibellius commented, "Pay no attention to what the critics say; there has never been set up a statue in honor of a critic" (2010).

Augustine and Atatürk – voices from the past

For scholars in the West, the literary signposts of history are familiar landmarks: *The Magna Carta*, Martin Luther's *The Ninety-Five Theses* and *On the Bondage of the Will*, Calvin's *Institutes of the Christian Religion*, Aurelius Augustine's *Confessions* and *City of God*, the French Revolution's *The Rights of Man and the Citizen*, Karl Marx's *Das Kapital* and *The Communist Manifesto*. These works launched new social realities by redefining the basic rules of the game. These works have also been thoroughly researched for centuries. A scholar who wishes to take a fresh look at how a document can redefine an entire social order would do well to consider material from outside of the western canon. Comparison and contrast, parallax from a different standpoint, could well yield fresh insights into the vital question of "how shall we then live?" in times of historical transformation.

A key document in the annals of 20th-century anti-colonial literature was Kemal Atatürk's *Six Day Speech*, a formal address to the Turkish Parliament in 1927. This speech and book redefined the public social order of the Turkish nation so emphatically that, as recently as 2005, a million people marched in the streets of İstanbul to support Atatürk's secular order. Also as recently as 2005, only one book-length scholarly examination of the *Six Day Speech* had been completed in the

English language. The combination of profound influence and insufficient prior attention makes this document, known to its Turkish public as *Nutuk*, worthy of further study.

We can usefully compare Atatürk, a 20th-century secular Muslim, to Augustine, a 5th-century African Christian. Both men addressed the challenge of a collapsing imperial social order. Both were midwives of a stable successor civilization. Both encapsulated their achievements, and achieved their long-range influence, with book-length documents. Both were successful world re-makers. Both men inaugurated new social realities. Augustine and Atatürk both gave those who heeded them a new frame of reference, a new map of the world to orient themselves by, and a new sense of destiny to guide their lives and aspirations.

What kinds of meaningful commonalities could be found between Nutuk and Augustine's *City of God*, created in different eras and for different audiences? Each defined a meaningful new social order in the aftermath of societal implosion. Can we learn relevant lessons by comparing these two works? Can societal patterns defined 4,000 years ago be used to extract the most enduring lessons from these documents?

The purpose of this study is to seek answers to these questions. We will examine how these two blueprints handled the persuasive themes they shared, beginning with a survey of relevant literature in chapter 2 of this study.

Because of the vast contrasts of the contexts and perspectives that shaped the minds of Atatürk and Augustine, the themes these two unlikely partners had in common should come into sharper focus. In chapter 3, we will examine these two books through the five-point covenant model proposed by Meredith Kline, and later refined by other Calvinist scholars. This comparative analysis should help us learn more about how one man can rhetorically re-arrange the universe for tens of millions of people.

In chapter 4, we will explore the ways a computer-aided quantitative textual analysis of Nutuk can lend support to the insights developed in the earlier chapters.

Finally, in Chapter 5, we will discuss the implications of the themes highlighted by our qualitative and quantitative analyses. We will also consider the autobiographical motives for this paper.

Responses to social collapse

Sometimes, societies lose their bearings, their morale, and their confidence. These can be "teachable moments" for later scholars as well as for the people in the crux of that experience. When all is going well, there is little interest in alternate ways of arranging one's life, work, or culture. Augustine and Atatürk addressed times when things were not going well. Social orders are resilient. As long as "the man in the street" embraces the "metaphysical dream" his culture uses to justify its own existence, a given society can endure, and overcome, terrible setbacks (Weaver, 1984, p. 18). However, if the hero story, the most widely embraced "grand metanarrative" at the culture's heart, is discredited, the people inside that world experience the end of their world (Gellert, 2001, p. 4). The "chattering classes" usually respond with panicked jeremiads, or learned inquests. "The owl of Minerva takes its flight only when the shades of night are gathering," wrote Hegel (2008, p. xxi). A social order's dynamics are only completely summarized toward the end of that society.

Aristotle called man "a political animal." Apart from participation in the community, this ancient said, people are less than fully human (Aristotle, Book I, ch. II). Humans normally live in a social order. Hermits, and autism sufferers, are the exceptions that stress-test this rule.

The *fin de siècle* motif attracts attention, especially during uncertain times. Edward Gibbon took up residence in "the grandeur that was Rome" as his shelter from Elizabethan turmoil (Gibbon, 1898, p. 215). In the 1930s, Lev Nussimbaum became Essad Bey, *The Orientalist*, and converted to Islam as a gesture of homesick yearning for the perceived stability of the vanished Ottoman Empire (Reiss, 2006). Isaac Asimov reprised Gibbon's work on a galactic scale, with several *Foundations* standing in for the medieval monasteries that husbanded, and then re-ignited the flame of civilization (2004).

Why this enduring fascination with societies pushed beyond endurance? Perhaps, it is because innate qualities are best revealed by tests. When concrete test cylinders are compressed to the breaking point, the technician has insight into the durability of the bridge deck. When large-scale communities lose their cohesion and their sense of identity, the attentive observer may detect valid information about the nature of community in general.

The collapse of social orders is a regular event in history. The phoenix rise of new orders from the ashes of the old, however, is a rarer phenomenon. When the miracle of cultural regeneration happens, though, the key documents that define the new orders are not created by the hand-wringing observers, but by the participants in the societal transformations. This redefinition, if successful, is usually encoded in a seminal text. For example, Luther may have launched a Reformation with his *Ninety-Five Theses*, but it is John Calvin who further systematized and codified the transformation with his *Institutes of the Christian Religion*. A researcher examining the role of seminal documents in crystallizing new social constructions of reality could even study the fiction of the era on the cusp. Times of transition are often times of frantic creativity. As Harry Lime, the central character in Orson Wells' movie *The Third Man* said:

> In Italy for thirty years under the Borgias they had warfare, terror, murder and bloodshed but they produced Michelangelo, Leonardo da Vinci and the Renaissance. In Switzerland, they had brotherly love; they had five hundred years of democracy and peace and what did that produce? The cuckoo clock. (Reed, 1949)

For those who do not bow at the altar of chaos, however, it makes more sense to examine, compare, and analyze writings that actually shape the inner workings of the new orders. Truly influential documents respond to real events, and call forth profound insights from exemplars of the transformed society. To persuade people to embrace a new set of ground rules you need a personal charisma that appeals to the deepest yearnings of the readers, in order to bring them to see the logic of the new perspective.

Atatürk and his Nutuk and Augustine and his *City of God* offer a meaningful opportunity to conduct such analysis and make such comparisons. Both men were products of cultures that had lost social order. Both designed stable, but radically different, new shared perceptions of social order. Each man helped an empire make the transition to something else. In both cases, the transformation was encoded in a significant document. If we can analyze exemplars from radically different backgrounds that nonetheless yield similar results, a careful examination may well lead to fresh insights into shared elements of the communal human experience.

An understudied, overlooked masterpiece

Political texts can yield relevant insights that transcend their immediate context. In 1927, Atatürk, the father of modern Turkey, addressed his nation's Grand National Assembly for six consecutive days, speaking for six hours a day. This "Gigantic Lecture" (Büyük Nutuk) discredited the prior civil, political, and religious order. It then defined the outlines of a new national order. Eight decades later, Nutuk still offers grist for the communications scholar's little mill. How do we explain the impact of this work, the enduring power of the concepts that redefined a nation? This "Turkish Magna Carta" cries out for rigorous attention, given its importance in world history. As of 2005, only one scholarly book-length analysis of this speech or lecture was available in the English language, Aysel Morin's doctoral dissertation "Crafting A Nation: The Mythic Construction Of The New Turkish National Identity In Atatürk's Nutuk." As the Turkish nation that Atatürk defined begins to question the terms of that definition, the time seems right for us to look again at this landmark document.

A metaphor

Esperanto provides a useful metaphor for the Turkish experience. This hobbyist language has only one definite article and no grammatical gender. All the nouns end in o, the adjectives in a, the adverbs in e. The available verb forms are ruthlessly condensed to five forms – past, present, future, imperative, and conditional. The verb *sori*, to soar, can only become soris, soras, Soros, soru, or sorus.[2] The Turkish transition from a traditional, heterogeneous empire to a

---

[2] Nearly a century ago, a Hungarian Jewish family decided to assimilate. As is traditional in these cases, they chose a new family name – the future tense of the Esperanto verb *sori* (to soar).

compact modern state provides an Esperanto for research into social transformation. The components are all functional, all in place, but in a simplified, condensed, and accessible form. According to one Turkish scholar, her nation's "coming of age" compressed into ten years the developments that Western nations needed four centuries to absorb (Morin, 2004, p. 284).

The Turks, Morin writes, deserve attention since they exercised an influence out of proportion to their numbers in the world's "history, politics, and culture" while founding more than a hundred states and empires over 1,500 years of continuous history (Morin, 2004, p. 21). This latest development in their long story has relevance for societies in transition today.

The Turkish experience lets us examine a dramatic social transformation within one nation and linguistic community. Even Turks who disagree with Atatürk's atheism regard this charismatic leader as the indispensable agent of that transformation. These changes were then reported on by that leader, who happened to be a gifted teacher, in one major document. "The writing of history is as important as the making of it," wrote Kemal Atatürk, a man who did both (Atatürk, 2010).

Brief description of Nutuk

In 1924, the Treaty of Lausanne formalized an anomaly. The victors of the War to End All Wars reluctantly admitted that one defeated power had refused to stay defeated. The "sick man of Europe" would not politely stay on his putative deathbed, let alone become an organ donor. The Turks refused to have their homeland dismembered on the basis of secret agreements crafted in European salons (Mears, 1924, p. 556). In an epic effort with few parallels in history, the Turkish people rallied, took on the combined military might of England, France, Italy, and Greece, fought invading armies to a standstill, and then hurled the intruders out of their homeland, ballet skirts, pom-poms, and all (Hemingway, 1936).

This national epic became a new Iliad from old Troy's neighborhood. Some sagas summarize a culture's soul and enter the historical record as epic poetry. *The Epic of Gilgamesh* meditates on disaster, survival, personal greatness, friendship, and death (Sandars, 1972). *Beowulf* presents an exemplar, an epitome of a Saxon knight, Christian, and warrior (Podles, 2004, pp. 92-99). The *Iliad* and the *Odyssey* encapsulate the defining characteristics of Bronze Age Greece. Atatürk's Nutuk is a similar time capsule, preserving for later ages a vivid glimpse into a freeze-framed moment of national, cultural, and social transformation.

This document at the heart of modern Turkish national identity, Nutuk, takes the form of a classroom lecture on political, military, and diplomatic history, a long-winded, didactic oral presentation. Kemal Atatürk spent three months preparing this speech, assembling, selecting, and incorporating the documents at his disposal. As he dictated the record of his legacy, he would sometimes work for twenty-four hours straight, take a brief nap, then resume (Kinross, 1965, p. 499).

The winners usually write the history books. At least, the winners select the material that goes into the history books. Some winners select material they wrote to go into the history books. Finally, every now and then, the winners select the material that they wrote concerning events that they consummated to go into the history books.

Julius Caesar's *The Gallic Wars* kept his name and deeds before the Roman populace and its kingmakers. So too did Dwight

Eisenhower's *Crusade in Europe*. Richard Nixon wrote a number of books describing his perspective on events of his day. And, just to make sure history got all the details right, Nixon taped his conversations with other movers and shakers.

Nutuk, one of the key documents of 20th-century nationalism, can be accused of solipsism. This "six day speech," delivered to the Turkish general assembly in October 1927 by Mustafa Kemal Atatürk, father of the modern Turkish republic, is largely comprised of source material he created. Yet, beyond any cavils, the fact of the Turkish Republic remains. For more than 80 years, a society once dreaded as a backwards oriental despotism has stood proudly on the world stage as a respected modern nation-state. A grateful nation gave the name Atatürk (father of the Turks) to the soldier-scholar who made it happen. To this day, Turks regard Nutuk as the foundation document of their social order (Morin, 2004, p. 20).

Significance of this study

Disintegrating nations can be dangerous to themselves and others, producing, as Mark Twain said, "more history than can be consumed locally" (as cited in Sampson, 1999). Islam has dominated the news ever since September 11, 2001. Once again, the world wonders if a nation can combine Islamic values with western norms. And once again, the significance and success of the Turkish Republic attracts notice.

People can transcend toxic memes, if given the right tools, the right diagnostic and repair manuals. Every religion has its fringe elements. However, for nearly eight decades, the Republic of Turkey has found ways to keep the dangerous elements of Islam bottled up. During this time, a policy of *Yurta sûlh, cihanda sûlh* (Peace at home, peace abroad) has made them good neighbors to surrounding nations, de-facto allies of Israel, and staunch friends of America throughout the Cold

War. Turkish women are the best-educated in the Muslim world, and received the franchise years before women in a number of other European nations (Morin, 2004, p. 55).

Credit for this is due to Kemal Atatürk. To this day, the people of Turkey revere Atatürk as a combination George Washington, Thomas Jefferson, and George Mason. Morin cites several scholars whose academic work supports the Turkish belief that Atatürk is almost completely and personally responsible for the existence of modern Turkey, a one-man distillation of all the American founding fathers (2004, p. 20).

Atatürk used the political capital gained as "savior of the nation" to persuade millions of people to transfer their allegiance from the linchpins of an Islamic social order to a secular national state. In October 1927 Atatürk spent six days explaining to the National Assembly the nature of his achievements. Nutuk's concluding exhortation to "the youth of Turkey" hangs, framed, on schoolhouse walls and in government offices. It has been memorized and recited by generations of schoolchildren.

Societies can transform themselves, given the proper catalysts. A careful examination of the effective instruments of such a transformation can help the scholar understand the critical questions that must be answered by those who would make an enduring difference in their worlds.

Nutuk was chosen for review since it presents the transformative events through the eyes and words of the acknowledged primary agent of Turkey's transformation. Nutuk includes the information that the significant gentleman considered significant.

The primary source document used in this study is an English translation of Nutuk published online at

27

http://www.interaktifokul.com/english/Nutuk/Nutuk.asp.
This text was extracted on March 3, 2006 from the web pages
using python script Nutuk.py created by David Coblentz. The
web site creator performed an optical character recognition
(OCR) scan of a printed English translation and uploaded this
text into 611 discrete files, one per source page. The python
scripts downloaded the text of each page and saved it as a
numbered ASCII text file.

An English translation was used since the original document
was created in Ottoman Turkish ("Osmanlı"), a court
language composed of roughly equal parts Turkish (a Ural-
Altaic language), Arabic (from the Semitic language family),
and Persian (Indo-European). Only specialized scholars read
Osmanlı in this century, and even native Turkish speakers
usually read Nutuk in translation (G. Lewis, 2002).

This study will compare Nutuk to another document that
helped an overwhelmed imperial people come to terms with
the destruction of their empire and to embrace a new social
order, Augustine's *City of God*. The assumption is that
documents which achieved a similar effect share similar
components.

Brief description of The City of God

Augustine's major work, *The City of God*, was inspired by the
devastating events of 410 AD, when Alaric the Goth sacked
Rome. This was a blow to the heart of the Roman Empire's
corporate identity. Some contemporary writers, thinkers, and
orators blamed the Christian religion for undermining the
traditional values that Rome had embraced in her times of
greatness. The most noteworthy of these *J'accuse* documents
came from the quill of Varro. In order to refute the polemics
and philippics of this apologist for classical paganism,
Augustine, bishop of Hippo in North Africa, wrote his

magnum opus. In twenty-two books, *The City of God* drags the obsolete and decrepit former order before the bar of history, and offers a new way of understanding one's place in the universe. The old Rome, formed by a love of self to the exclusion of God, is being supplanted by the new Rome, the city of God, formed by the love of God and neighbor. Since this document so powerfully influenced the western European perspective on corporate life for more than a thousand years, we will use it as our epitome, our gold standard.

Augustine and Atatürk both served as undertakers to an older order, laying it decently to rest. By the time each had finished his work, the people they influenced with their rhetoric no longer considered a pagan empire, or an Islamic empire, a suitable and pragmatic vessel for their corporate hopes. Each of these thought leaders served as midwife to a new civic order, a new way of triangulating one's location in the universe of gods and men. Together, they have something to teach those who study the mechanics of personal persuasion and social transformation.

In the next chapter, we will take a closer look at these two documents, and briefly discuss a body of communication theory that provides a basis for comparison.

Chapter 2: Literature Review

We will review several areas of literature particularly relevant to this study in this chapter. The bottom line: the words we use define the world we live in. Or, to impress scholars, you would say "the social and linguistic construction of reality is the essence of a social order."

Next, we will briefly parse Augustine's work and influence so that we can use these as a model, a yardstick, a standard of evaluation for a more detailed examination of Atatürk's place in history. We will look at the *context* of the City of God: an empire that had just suffered a massive loss of credibility. We will consider those characteristics that made Augustine a *catalyst* for the world that came after him. We will look at his *codex*, the literary distillation of his life's vision, his life's work. Finally, we will consider the *consequences* of his work, and how *The City of God* defined the core of Europe for the next thousand years.

Then, to provide an overview of Nutuk we will apply this same pattern, describing the context, catalyst, codex, and consequences of this more recent history-reporting and history-making document.

Social Construction of Reality

Augustine and Atatürk both thought the unthinkable, about the shape of life after the loss of the civic container that had shaped the lives of their peers. Every social order is a linguistically constructed perception of reality that both defines, and is defined by, those who participate in it. Communication research continues to provide insights into the shared understandings that bind communities together.

Humans normally live in a social order. Aristotle wrote:

And when many villages so entirely join themselves together as in every respect to form but one society, that society is a city, and contains in itself, if I may so speak, the end and perfection of government: first founded that we might live, but continued that we may live happily. . . . Hence it is evident that a city is a natural production, and that man is naturally a political animal, and that whosoever is naturally and not accidentally unfit for society, must be either inferior or superior to man: thus the man in Homer, who is reviled for being "without society, without law, without family." Such a one must naturally be of a quarrelsome disposition, and as solitary as the birds. (1495/1912, Book I, ch. II)

Even as Athena sprang full-grown from the forehead of Zeus, Aristotle's hypothetical ideal city apparently just showed up. It has no point of reference beyond itself. In contrast to Aristotle's position, most traditional social orders view themselves as patterned after some transcendent archetype. The "Sumerian King's List" speaks of the primordial days "when kingship was let down from heaven" (Saggs, 2000, p. 59). From the dawn of literacy, humanity has embraced the idea that social order is an earthly replica of a pre-existing condition. In poetic imagery of poignant beauty, the gospel writer John described the new order that emerged with the coming of Jesus Christ as a new city, a heavenly Jerusalem that, like the Sumerian kingship, was lowered from heaven (Rev. 3:13; 21:2-3).

However, civilization has always had its discontents. Nietzsche's final published work, *The Antichrist*, asserts that heroic individuals can rise above the hobbling constraints of petty ethical systems to create, through sheer self-will, new realities (1918). Ana, in G. B. Shaw's play *Man and Superman*, crosses herself and devoutly implores the universe to send her a father to *The Superman* (Shaw, 1959, p. 144). More recently,

Aslan Reza defines the essence of modernism as the notion that we are free to invent our own social orders. We are no longer the products of our societies, but can order up new social orders at whim (Reza, 2009, p. 132).

Berger and Luckmann's landmark book *The Social Construction of Reality* (1967) demonstrated the extent to which the reality we experience is a cooperative verbal construct. To participate in a community, people need to have a shared vocabulary, a shared grammar of social order. Mention a few words, a catch phrase, and the other party will immediately recall a whole context, a whole concept cluster. Every coherent order has its handful of such "dictionaries."

The ramblings of schizophrenics would make sober sense if prefaced with the explanation "I dreamed..." Berger and Luckmann explain that few of us find it a problem to distinguish between dreams and waking reality (1967). However, common-sense, every-day, waking reality is not as self-evident as it seems at first glance, but is actually a construct composed in cooperation with the social order around us.

The prototypical axiom, the foundation, the archetype for all communication, is the face-to-face encounter. This is the most information-dense interface. The combination of verbal and nonverbal communication allows two people to enter into each others' worlds, despite limits to insight based on social factors and personality traits. Language permits us to translate our thoughts, feelings, and intentions into transferable tokens. The words are not the same as the items signified, but they are far easier to share.

Society as objective reality

We create the social realities we live in by means of language. "As soon as one observes phenomena that are specifically human, one enters the realm of the social" (Berger & Luckmann, 1967, p. 51).

Berger and Luckmann refrain from value judgments, but observation suggests that the communities wordsmiths create can be functional or dysfunctional. It would appear that certain institutions, certain enduring covenantal relations, are hard-wired into the human system, and cannot be violated with impunity for long. When a culture's leaders and opinion makers are insulated from the results of their actions, the severed feedback loop can result in the perpetuation of harmful and unsustainable policies, but only for a limited period of time (Sowell, 1995, pp. 94, 247-250).

Berger and Luckmann point out how difficult it can be to transfer a social structure to another generation (1967). The American Puritans who landed at Plymouth Rock in 1619 had the fervor to break free from comfortable lives and to endure the loss of more than half of their members during the first hard winter. The next generation, however, did not feel the same intense fervor. The "half-way covenant" provided for the children of those who did not know themselves to be among the elect. Neither this practice, nor the railing "jeremiads," kept the culture from slipping *From Puritan to Yankee* (Bushman, 1980).

However, there are ways to transmit culture, by externalizing and institutionalizing it. If the elders of one Mennonite community decree that two suspenders are too worldly, their heirs will still be wearing a single diagonal suspender a century later (J. Menno, personal communication, 1973).

Communities that wish to transmit their values typically assign special times and specialists the task of doing so, and making the lessons stick. For example, German children are, on ceremonial occasions, led around a boundary marker three times by the ear (Barnhart, 2004).

Social structures are also sustained by people with specific and specialized roles. These roles can have varying degrees of relevance to the culture as a whole, or even to their stated purposes. Freemasons wear aprons and use the emblems of tools, but rarely carve stone.

"Reification" refers to the natural tendency to regard these institutions as self-existing, apart from those who create and inhabit them. This is especially the case when the social entity is created by a highly specialized subset of general society (Berger & Luckmann, 1967, p. 95). The cliché "You can't fight city hall" refers to the estrangement people sense between themselves and their leaders. A comparable Turkish proverb *İt ürür kervan yürür* (the dogs bark, but the caravan moves on) also refers to this sense of alienation from society's movers and shakers and their clubs.

A social order's "legitimation" starts with kin and works its way out to symbolic universes, full-scale explanations about "life, the universe, and everything." Legitimation establishes the credibility of social institutions horizontally, across the broad spectrum of those affected, and vertically, throughout individual life spans (Berger & Luckmann, 1967, pp. 94-95). The justifications for these groups range from simple explanations ("Because I say so") all the way up to complete symbol systems. These symbolic universes provide identity to the members of the affected cultures, and suppress disturbing counter-trends. They dispute the sanity of unbelievers, and provide "therapy" for those whose faith is wavering. The word masters who manage the definitions of these symbolic universes can annoy the practitioners of various arts and sciences by claiming to have a better grasp of the root purposes they are pursuing than the craftsmen and artisans themselves enjoy. In extreme cases, these masters of symbolic universes become *intelligentsia*, the alienated pontificators who live on a marginal level while resentfully re-ordering the social order in their imaginations (Berger & Luckmann, 1967, pp. 125-126). Sometimes, these social theoreticians acquire power, and succeed half-way in their effort to create heaven and hell on earth, by re-ordering society to fit their Procrustean logic.

However, history tells of a handful of readers and writers, thinkers and doers, who provide fresh answers to old questions, more wholesome paradigms that permit life to go on in the face of apparently overwhelming challenges. Under Atatürk's leadership, the Turkish people absorbed the loss of an empire, repelled scavenging armies, and built a modern secular republic that boldly assumed its place in the sun. How did Atatürk rally a defeated nation to shake off adversity and create a new order? How did Augustine open the eyes of those whose world was shattered to see fresh hope, fresh possibilities, beyond the immediate disaster? Perhaps, both men played on the same keys, and pounded on some of the same basic themes that resonate with human aspirations.

Society as subjective reality.

Berger and Luckmann distinguish between primary and secondary socialization. Parents comprise almost the entire environment of their children, and do the most to impart language, manners, and the other tools children need to navigate through social reality (1967). For example, the chief school psychologist of Anchorage, Alaska, Mark Smedley, PhD, reports that children adopted from Russian orphanages, where they typically spent their first few years in cribs, devoid of human interaction, tend to have delayed development, and often become unmanageable upon reaching puberty (Smedley, 2000).

Secondary socialization involves more specialized knowledge and skills, usually imparted by a specialist, and added to the primary socialization.

Re-socialization involves the subjugation of some aspects of primary socialization in order for a new set of imperatives to be imparted. This can induce conflicts. Research on the social maturity of home-educated children indicated that white, middle-class fundamentalist children attending public school had far below-average levels of social maturity. The process of re-socialization appeared, in their case, to have adverse effects (Smedley, 1992). "(T)here are discrepancies between primary and secondary socialization" (Berger & Luckmann, 1967, p. 171).

Frequently, these impositions and expectations are justified by a shared appeal to an overarching frame of reference. "History," Napoleon Bonaparte said, "is the version of past events that people have decided to agree upon" (Bonaparte, 2009). Novelist Lois McMaster Bujold has one of her characters muse, "And yet it seemed to work for them, somehow. They made it work. Pretending a government into existence. Perhaps all governments were such consensus fictions, at their heart" (Bujold, 1999, p. 297).

Communication scholars wrestle with these kinds of questions, since the focus of our interest is upon the interactions that create community, define community, and define us as members of our communities. We can enrich our theories by boiling them in the test tube of history. We apply our theories to communication artifacts, consider the results, and then refine the theories. A 20th-century Middle-Eastern Muslim and a 5th-century African Christian each created viable social redefinitions while in the crucible of massive societal disintegration. One redefinition endured for more than a thousand years, and still influences scholars and statesmen. The other paradigm is beginning to fray around the edges. Perhaps we can learn something about what Atatürk did right by comparing his magnum opus to Augustine's. At the conclusion of this study, we will have a few suggestions for those who create and nurture the social bonds to consider.

Augustine

Context.

In 410 AD, Alaric the Goth invaded the city of Rome, the eternal city, the source, hub, and master of a vast empire. This was a devastating blow to those millions of people in diverse lands who viewed themselves, first of all, as Romans. Thomas Merton writes, "Rome had been the inviolate mistress of the world for a thousand years. The fall of the city that some had thought would stand forever demoralized what was left of the civilized world" (Augustine, 1961, p. ix).

The pagan writers were deeply troubled, and frequently blamed Christianity for undermining the traditional faith, the traditional morality, and the traditional prowess of Rome. The most eloquent of these, the philosopher Varro, caught the attention of Augustine, and motivated him to begin writing *The City of God* in order to refute this most articulate and visible adversary of the Christian cause.

Yet even the Christian subjects of Rome often viewed their public identities as indivisible composites of Christian and Roman. Historian Eusebius viewed the conversion and career of Constantine with nearly apocalyptic enthusiasm, as heralding the beginning of a new age, when the might and majesty of the Great City would be domesticated and harnessed to the purposes of the Christian gospel (Eusebius, 1990).

37

Augustine's older contemporary Christian writer, Jerome, the translator of the Vulgate Latin Bible, had fled the temptations of the imperial city for the safer solitudes of the Judean desert. He reacted to the news of Rome's fall, however, as one whose world had crumbled:

> I will keep silence concerning the rest, lest I seem to despair of the mercy of God. For a long time, from the Black Sea to the Julian Alps, those things which are ours have not been ours; and for thirty years, since the Danube boundary was broken, war has been waged in the very midst of the Roman Empire. Our tears are dried by old age. Except a few old men, all were born in captivity and siege, and do not desire the liberty they never knew.

> Who could believe this? How could the whole tale be worthily told? How Rome has fought within her own bosom not for glory, but for preservation – nay, how she has not even fought, but with gold and all her precious things has ransomed her life . . .

> Who could believe that Rome, built upon the conquest of the whole world, would fall to the ground? That the mother herself would become the tomb of her peoples? That all the regions of the East, of Africa and Egypt, once ruled by the queenly city, would be filled with troops of slaves and handmaidens? That to-day holy Bethlehem should shelter men and women of noble birth, who once abounded in wealth and are now beggars?" (Jerome, n.d.)

From the Italian peninsula to the remote hermitage on the fringes of the empire, the people whose identity was formed as Romans felt the shock as a deeply personal catastrophe.

Catalyst.

Augustine, an African Christian, described the forging of his character in his classic work *Confessions*. He was born in 354, the son of a Christian mother and pagan father. When Augustine demonstrated early scholastic ability, his parents sacrificed to further his education, sending him to the best local schools, and later on to Rome. His father took pride in his abilities, and his mother overindulged his wild streak. For example, in keeping with the belief of the time that sins committed after baptism were more heinous than those before, they withheld the sacrament from him, even when he begged to be baptized after a serious childhood illness.

Much of Augustine's young manhood was spent in the Manichean heresy, a religious movement that portrayed reality in stark, dark, dualistic terms: Matter and procreation are bad; spiritual contemplation is good; everyone should be a celibate vegetarian. As a teacher of rhetoric, he used his influence to bring others into this cult as well.

A number of influences, Christian and otherwise, brought about his deliverance from the cult. A famed Manichean teacher, Faustas, proved to be thoroughly disappointing in person. Faustas proclaimed as doctrine things about nature that were demonstrably false.

By 384 AD, Augustine attracted notice from influential people in the Roman provincial capital of Milan. As a *rhetor*, a scholar, lawyer, and orator, he epitomized his culture's ideal of what a man of influence and refinement should be. Had not his conversion intervened, his gifts could have led to a career as a provincial governor. Cicero's *Hortensius* intensified Augustine's hunger for things of the spirit. Finally, in 386 AD, the erudite sermons of Ambrose, bishop of Milan, opened his eyes to the credibility of the Bible (O'Meara, 1973, p. 13).

A prolonged season of internal struggles ensued, documented with painful sincerity in Augustine's *Confessions*. Marcus Aurelius might address his sterile, austere, stoic *Meditations* to his own soul. Aurelius Augustine, by contrast, addressed his confessions to his God with the passion of an intoxicated lover. In one of the most famous conversion moments in literature, Augustine's internal turmoil was encountered, and resolved, by a providential intervention. His own words are cited here at length to provide additional insight into the character and motivations of this sage, scholar, and lover:

> I cast myself down I know not how, under a certain fig-tree, giving full vent to my tears; and the floods of mine eyes gushed out an acceptable sacrifice to Thee. And, not indeed in these words, yet to this purpose, spake I much unto Thee: and Thou, O Lord, how long? how long, Lord, wilt Thou be angry for ever? Remember not our former iniquities, for I felt that I was held by them. I sent up these sorrowful words: How long, how long, "to-morrow, and tomorrow?" Why not now? why not is there this hour an end to my uncleanness?

> So was I speaking and weeping in the most bitter contrition of my heart, when, lo! I heard from a neighbouring house a voice, as of boy or girl, I know not, chanting, and oft repeating, "Take up and read; Take up and read." . . . So checking the torrent of my tears, I arose; interpreting it to be no other than a command from God to open the book, and read the first chapter I should find. . . . Eagerly then I returned to the place where Alypius was sitting; for there had I laid the volume of the Apostle when I arose thence. I seized, opened, and in silence read that section on which my eyes first fell: *Not in rioting and drunkenness, not in chambering and wantonness, not in strife and envying; but put ye on the Lord Jesus Christ, and make not provision for the flesh, in concupiscence.* No further would I read; nor needed I: for instantly at the end of

this sentence, by a light as it were of serenity infused into my heart, all the darkness of doubt vanished away. (Augustine, 1961, p. 131)

The focus of his affections and the direction of his life were immediately transformed. Augustine dismissed his mistress and gave himself to studying the Christian religion with the intense attention that had brought him so far in his secular career. Two years after his conversion, Augustine and his circle of friends returned to Africa (Augustine, 1961, pp. 7-8). Three years later, in 391 AD, he was ordained to the priesthood. In 396 AD, he was elected Bishop of Hippo. As a faithful shepherd of his people, he engaged in their struggles, and vigorously resisted the encroachments of heterodox teachings. Donatists and Pelagians felt the sting of his tart, erudite pen. Even as David first overcame the lion and the bear, this shepherd's early conflicts prepared him for the largest struggle of his life (O'Meara, 1973, p. 8).

Codex.

Three years after Alaric sacked Rome, in 413 AD, Augustine began writing his apologia to counter the charges of the pagan critics. Marcellinus, a Christian friend of high social standing, had introduced him to Volusian, a pagan Roman magistrate with an open mind and a pragmatic approach to life. Volusian was well aware of the role paganism played in providing a stable shared culture for the Roman Empire, and needed to be assured that Christianity was up to the job of replacing an entire culture. Although the putative target of Augustine's apologetic was Varro, he also addressed every persuadable, responsible, pagan person of stature.

Augustine spent thirteen years, and 22 books issued in installments, refuting the pretentious claims of pagan Rome.

Out of respect for his adversary, Augustine does deal at some length with the apologetic technique Varro used of dividing theology into three parts: the mythical for the poets, the physical for the philosophers, and the civil for the proper ordering of the city (City VI, 5). A modern reader is reminded of Gibbon's comment: "The various modes of worship, which prevailed in the Roman world, were all considered by the people, as equally true; by the philosopher, as equally false; and by the magistrate, as equally useful" ("Edward Gibbon," n.d., para. 2).

Beginning with Book XI, Augustine addresses himself to his major theme, the existence of two cities. Books XI through XIV dealt with the origin of man, books XV through XVIII with history since creation, and books XIX through XXII with the diverse destinies of the two cities, and their citizens.

The core theme of *The City of God* is the new Jerusalem, the new society, the new corporate entity – God's elect people. Even as the Old Rome was characterized by a love of self to the contempt of God, so the New Rome was shaped by a love of God that placed all other loves on a lower plane (City XIV, c. 28). Even as the Old Rome was a human construct, prone to human sins and frailties and catastrophes, the New Rome, the New City, was preserved by its Founder and Captain for eternity. The turmoil and tragedies of human history simply threshed the pure grain of God's kingdom, purging God's people, God's city, of lingering corruption and sins. The sorrows of earthly life simply equipped the recipients of divine favor to better enjoy, and better fit into, their heavenly destiny.

Consequences.

O'Meara had an expansive view of Augustine's long-term influence, and wrote, "He set the mold in which Western Christendom was laid; he set it firmly and he set it fully. . . .

The thought patterns, determining action for fifteen hundred years, were set (not initiated, let it be noted) by him" (1973, p. 12).

Monk and mystic Thomas Merton had a more personalized vision of this book's influence, asserting that it celebrated the eschatological certainty that all of history would culminate, in the end, in an eternal state of felicity in Christ (City, p. xv).

Politically speaking, Augustine envisioned the new order as living a parallel existence to any and all temporary, temporal societies:

> This heavenly city, then, while it sojourns on earth, calls citizens out of all nations, and gathers together a society of pilgrims of all languages, not scrupling about diversities in the manners, laws, and institutions whereby earthly peace is secured and maintained, but recognizing that, however various these are, they all tend to one and the same end of earthly peace. (City XIX, 19)

Yes, existing kingdoms have their value and their place. However, no human political order may ever again claim the kind of overarching allegiance that the old Rome demanded. In one of his most enduring metaphors, Augustine compared human governments to criminal syndicates:

> Justice being taken away, then, what are kingdoms but great robberies? For what are robberies themselves, but little kingdoms? The band itself is made up of men; it is ruled by the authority of a prince, it is knit together by the pact of the confederacy; the booty is divided by the law agreed on. If, by the admittance of abandoned men, the evil increases to such a degree that it holds places, fixes abodes, takes possession of cities, and subdues people, it assumes the more plainly the name of a kingdom, because the reality is now manifestly

conferred on it, not by the removal of covetousness, but by the addition of impunity. (City IV, 4)

Augustine made thinkable the possibility that kings might not have unlimited power, unlimited rights. John Calvin, in the famous Book XX of his *Institutes of the Christian Religion*, affirms the dignity of earthly rulers, with the caveat that lesser magistrates have the right, even the duty, to resist the tyrannical enactments of unjust kings (Calvin, 2010). Although King James I viewed himself as "a species of divinity," a demigod by virtue of the crown on his head, the royal son Charles was beheaded for that same arrogance.

Human governments which disregard God's justice are simply larger criminal gangs. This belief lies at the root of Western liberties. A wholesome skepticism on the part of subjects can restrain the worst excesses of rulers who take themselves too seriously. On the other hand, nations that lose their sense of vital connection to the City of God, the eternal order, have time after time followed the siren's song of would-be earthly deities, such as Robespierre, Wilson, Mussolini, and Hitler.

This is a brief look at Augustine's life and work. When the core of their social reality, Rome, the Eternal City, fell beneath the sandals of the barbarians, *The City of God* gave Augustine's readers the conceptual tools they needed to build a new social reality. The new world, the world no longer centered on the proud might of imperial Rome, could look to the heavenly city for its inspiration. The City of God, created in the Garden of Eden and enduring past the end of history, could provide a more durable, more enduring ark of safety for human aspirations. Even though politicians fail, Augustine taught, God is undismayed, and gladly provides a cohesive identity to his people.

We will now use the pattern of this analysis (context, catalyst, codex, consequences) to structure our overview of Atatürk's achievements.

Kemal Atatürk

Context: the last days of the Ottoman Empire

To readers in later generations, it appears that Czarist Russia, Weimer Germany, and 1970s Cambodia collapsed into disarray almost overnight. Other social orders experienced a long, debilitating "decline and fall." The context that gave Atatürk his opportunity to make history was the failure of the Ottoman Empire to compete successfully with Western rivals in the centuries after the European Renaissance. Orhan Pamuk, a Nobel prize-winning Turkish novelist, asserts that the West first began to pull ahead in the area of the arts (2008, p. 319). Breakthroughs in such techniques as perspective and representational realism intimidated the celebrants of Ottoman glory. The Pamuk novel *Benim Adım Kırmızı* (My Name is Red) revolves around the unsuccessful attempt of an ambitious miniaturist to break free of his own artistic tradition and ape the Italian style of portraiture (2002). Yet, this is not the whole story. The ambivalence of Islamic culture toward representational art must be weighed against its exultation of the verbal arts. Most of the greatest Ottoman rulers were also poets, Pamuk wrote. Ottoman court poetry followed stringent requirements, but the collected works of these savants and statesmen, their *divans*, are renowned museum pieces that epitomize a refined and highly developed artistic sensibility (Pamuk, 2008, p. 359). In his speeches, Kemal Atatürk tapped into that stream of cultural tradition, salting his speeches with poetry, proverbs, and memorable "sound bites." To this day, Turkish elementary education requires pupils to memorize Atatürk's aphorisms and proverbs (Atatürk, 2010).

45

Yet, for those with eyes to see, or maps to read, the decline of the Ottoman Empire was obvious. The borders were shrinking. Ungrateful subject peoples infected with the virus of nationalism created civic disorders of varying intensities. The parties in the Balkan Wars used barbed wire, trenches, and airplanes several years before the larger European powers turned these lethal toys on each other (Hall, 2000, pp. 65, 130).

Kemal Atatürk was unsparing in his contempt for Islam. To him, this tradition represented backwardness and uncouth barbarism. Islam, Atatürk felt, generated the scorn emanating from the European thinkers he idolized, identified with, and wished to be numbered among. Kinross reports Atatürk's humiliation during a visit to Sicily, as street urchins mocked his fez and threw lemon rinds at him (1965, p. 39). On another occasion, an emotional display of loud piety, or "fanatical ecstasy," by whirling dervishes at a railway station left him acutely embarrassed, ashamed of his people and their gullibility. He regarded Islam as an internal enemy more dangerous than foreign foes. People could learn from worthy competitors, but Islam, he felt, inculcated a fatalism, passivity, and superstitious resistance to all that was bright, modern, hopeful, and progressive (Kinross, 1965, p. 14).

An early 20th-century French writer, Andre Sevier, agreed with this perspective on Islam, especially as practiced by Arabs. He wrote, "If the mosque is without adornment, that is not from any pre-meditated design, but simply because the Arab is incapable of adorning it; it is bare like the desert, bare like the Bedouin brain" (1922, p. 59).

Sevier describes Islam as "a doctrine conceived in a barbarian brain for a nation of barbarians" (1922, p. 52). Islam, he wrote, fixed intellectual limits, beyond which the Muslim could not go without denying his faith (1922, p. 94).

46

Islam was not a torch, as had been claimed, but an extinguisher. Conceived in a barbarous brain for the use of a barbarous people, it was – and it remains – incapable of adapting itself to civilization. Wherever it has dominated, it has broken the impulse toward progress and checked the evolution of society. (Sevier, 1922, p. 153)

Ironically, Sevier ends his diatribe against Islam with words of commendation for the Turks, whose innate common sense seemed to represent a counterweight to the dangers of fanatical Arabic Islam (1922, p. 136).

Another contemporary of Atatürk's, Alexander Aaronsohn, was a Jewish settler conscripted at the onset of WWI to serve, as the title of his vivid memoir explains, *With the Turks in Palestine*. Modern warfare met oriental backwardness, with predictable results. The Jewish and Christian minorities suffered more from the depredations of their nominal protectors, the Ottoman-led Arabic military force, than they did from allied armies. In the name of requisitioning needed war supplies, the settlers were stripped of resources, including draft animals that later died by the thousands from neglect. The most disciplined troops in this conscript army, Jewish and Christian soldiers, were disarmed and used as slave labor to build roads. The small Turkish leadership cadre demonstrated a measure of superior professionalism, but occasionally took part in the "requisition" raids (Aaronsohn, 1916). It was in this setting, after participating in a victorious skirmish, that Atatürk looked at a companion and asked, "Will you be a man of the future, or a man of the past?" When the friend cast his vote for the future, Atatürk instructed him to eschew pillaging (Kinross, 1965, p. 29). Fatalism, even in the face of locust plagues, rendered the Muslim populations unwilling to defend their native soil in Lebanon and Palestine (Aaronsohn, 1916). Lowell Thomas traveled *With Laurence in Arabia* to report on the successful efforts of a well-funded British agent to lead small-scale guerrilla raids on Turkish infrastructure (Thomas, 1967).

Atatürk viewed the Islam of his day as a major source of Ottoman distress. A statistical look at present-day Islam, as practiced in the traditional Arabic world, suggests that his diagnosis may have been accurate. On the one hand, by following Atatürk's lead, the Turkish Republic became a progressive modern state with a literate populace, and a high rate of participation in the learned professions by Turkish women (Morin, 2004, p. 55). By contrast, the Arabic-speaking parts of the world, those which froze their culture, "kept the faith," and remained steadfast to their vision of Islamic life, demonstrate how things could have been far different, and far bleaker, for the Turkish people. Lieutenant Colonel James G. Lacey described a dysfunctional social order in his essay "The Impending Collapse of Arab Civilization" and wrote, "(T)he Muslim faith is flourishing. Arabs, however, most of whom are Muslims, are not" (2005).

Events seemed to demonstrate that 19th-century Islam, like 5th-century paganism, had failed as a viable foundation for social order. Obviously, to astute observers of the Turkish scene a century ago, a change had to be made. The continuing stability of the Turkish experiment suggests that real change, real progress, actually happened. This is a hopeful token for the larger geopolitical scene. Cultures can, given the right kind of inspiration, break free from crippling and dysfunctional paradigms in order to flourish in new ways.

Pre-existing modernizing trends.

Atatürk's words and deeds did build upon existing trends. In his book *The Imperial Classroom: Islam, the State, and Education in the Late Ottoman Empire*, Benjamin Fortna opens a window on a fascinating few decades of Turkish history. In the early 1880s, Abdul Hamid II, "the last sultan to rule as well as reign" (Fortna, 2002, p. 12), took alarm at the speed with which his homeland was losing its identity to modern trends (Finkel, 2005, pp. 490-500), and fought back in several ways. Most famously, he abolished the Turkish parliament. At a time when Turkish finances were in such disarray that they were managed by foreign bankers, his regime built nearly 10,000 modern schools within a few decades (Fortna, 2002, pp. 98-99). He hoped to resist the encroachment of Western materialism by rapidly building Western-style schools. To overcome the inertia of the peasantry, it was necessary, he believed, to wrest the education of the young from the hands of parents and local clergy.

Abdul Hamid II had reason to fear. Evangelical Christian missionaries brought their faith, funds, and schools to Anatolia. Ethnic minorities – Greeks, Armenians, Jews – educated their children in these schools to attain mastery and influence in the areas of commerce and business. The creedal and financial future of his nation was being deftly purloined, right under his nose (Fortna, 2002, pp. 79, 84).

Fortna does an excellent job of portraying the euphoria that surrounded this educational effort, the expectation that the French model of standardized curricula, leavened with Islamic instruction, could reverse his nation's decline. The Islam taught, however, would be the brand sanctioned by the Sublime Porte, rather than by the local hoca (Fortna, 2002, p. 101).

"Ottoman high culture was largely textual," Fortna points out (2002, p. 171), confirming Pamuk's description of the role poetry played in the development of the Ottoman statesman (2008, p. 359). This textual focus, however, did not prepare the students for the impact of maps. Although some fanatical

49

mobs assaulted schoolhouses, tore these "images" from the walls, and threw them into privies, the students began to see, in graphic imagery, the shrinking frontiers of the Ottoman Empire. Yes, they had a place in the larger world, but it was a diminishing place (Fortna, 2002, pp. 165, 198, 199).

However, the traditional Islamic reverence for education, for learning, when blended with the messianic expectations laden upon the modern school systems, conferred high prestige upon the teacher. Even today, when a student is called upon, he stands, and begins his answer with *Öğretmenim*, "My teacher" (Gökküşağı, 2004, p. 25).

Fortna makes a persuasive argument that the societal transformation wrought by Atatürk is simply a more dramatic instance of a rapprochement that had been underway for more than half a century. There were, he asserts, no "wild swings between secular and religious periods in the Late Ottoman and Republican eras" (2002, p. 247).

The Life of a Catalyst

Numerous studies of Atatürk, including Kinross (1965), Volkan and Itzkowitz (1984), Bozdag (2002), Macfie (1994), Mango (1999), and Sheldon (2000), argue for his significance as a leader. When Time magazine polled historians in 2000 to determine the most influential people of the 20th century, only Winston Churchill polled ahead of Atatürk, with 33.8% of the votes to 33.2% (Time, 2000).

Atatürk was born in the European city of Salonika in 1881, "within earshot of the Greek church bells below" and grew up in a cosmopolitan crossroads of diverse cultures (Kinross, 1965, p. 8). He resisted his mother's desire that he pursue an Islamic education, choosing instead to enter a military school at the age of 12. This was a wise move, since, as Kinross wrote:

(T)he officer class was the elite of the country. Its academies, subsidized by the Sultan, were nurseries of instruction, giving their pupils a grounding not only in military matters but in history, economic, philosophy. They were democratic institutions, composed of all social classes, in which it was possible to rise by ability and merit alone. (1965, p. 14)

A Turkish scholar summarizes Atatürk's military career:

During this gradual decline of his country, Mustafa Kemal chose a military career and started to serve the Ottoman army in various wars, namely the Italo-Turkish War of 1911-12 as well as the Balkan Wars of 1913, but more importantly in 1914 when the World War I broke out and Turkey decided to fight on the side of Germany. The Ottoman forces under his command could defeat British, French and Anzac and later Russian armies and such successive victories in defeating the Allied forces brought him power in the eyes of the sultanate and public. (Guler, 2007)

On a number of fronts, handicapped by haphazard logistics, Atatürk led his forces to victory after victory. At the beginning of the war, his outgunned forces combined inspiring leadership with the valor of the foot soldiers to hold Gallipolis against a combined Allied invasion force. His service in the Sultan's army culminated in a fighting retreat from Syria before Allenby's superior forces, in which Atatürk managed to preserve much in the way of men, munitions, and materiel. As Kinross wrote, "Thus, after four long disastrous years of war, Kemal emerged from the general carnage as the only Turkish commander without a defeat to his name" (1965, p. 151).

The end of the war revealed the perfidy of the European powers as well as the incompetence of the Ottoman leadership. The victorious nations were not in a magnanimous mood, as the Germans soon discovered. The Allies' intentions for the Turks were even more severe. Four secret agreements – the Constantinople agreement (1915), the Secret Treaty of London (1915), the Sykes-Picot Agreement (1916), and the St. Jean de Maurienne Agreement (1916) – were crafted in European salons. These colonizing nations were accustomed to dividing maps into negotiated spheres of influence that took no account of the peoples living in the mapped areas. It apparently made *realpolitik* sense to England and France to use chunks of Turkey to bribe Italy and Russia to enter the Great War on their side (Lewis, 1960, pp. 48-49; Kinross, 1965, p. 164).

The beaten and browbeaten politicians of İstanbul willingly consented to the dismemberment of their nation, in exchange for a consolation prize, a theme-park rump republic where they could reign, resplendent, with accustomed pomp and pageantry (Kinross, 1965, p. 183). Atatürk was dispatched to the hinterlands as an "inspector," tasked with the assignment of disarming his people. At this point, the Greeks invaded Smyrna, and provided the galvanizing event that gave Atatürk his opportunity. Winston Churchill describes what happened next, using his usual vivid and occasionally overblown prose:

> Loaded with follies, stained with crimes, rotted with misgovernment, shattered by battle, worn down by long disastrous wars, his Empire falling to pieces around him, the Turk was still alive. In his breast was beating the heart of a race that had challenged the world and for centuries had contended victoriously against all comers. In his hands was once again the equipment of a modern Army, and at his head a Captain who, with all that is learned of him, ranks with the four or five outstanding figures of the cataclysm. In the tapestried and gilded chambers of Paris were assembled the law-givers of the world. In Constantinople, under the guns of the allied Fleets there functioned a puppet

Government of Turkey. But among the stern hills and valleys of "the Turkish Homelands" in Anatolia, there dwelt that company of poor men . . . who would not see it settled so; and that their bivouac fires at this moment sat in the rags of a refugee the august spirit of Fair Play. (as cited in Ucuzsatar, 2002)

A corrupt and decrepit old empire was collapsing, while a new order struggled to be born. With the help of loyal telegraph operators, Atatürk directed the Turkish war of independence (1919-1922) as an "internet war," one managed, and recorded, using wired media. The primary historical account of these events, *Nutuk*, is largely composed of telegrams Atatürk sent and received. Using this electric medium, the midwife of the modern Turkish republic managed complex negotiations with allies and enemies at home and abroad. He motivated his forces, and kept before a desperate nation a vision of what they could hope to become, of what they were fighting for (Kinross, 1965, p. 221).

To maintain national order, Atatürk convened a Grand National Assembly in Ankara, near the Anatolian heartland, far removed from the compromises and corruptions of İstanbul. He resigned from the Sultan's forces, and had himself commissioned by this new representative government of the nation. He enlisted the loyalty of the nation, requiring each household to participate in the struggle for national salvation by providing the soldiers with "a contribution for the forces of a parcel of linen, a pair of socks, and a pair of shoes." Draft animals were conscripted, and peasant women drove ox carts to the battlefront (Kinross, 1965, p. 311).

Unlike earlier leaders who governed by remote control, Atatürk also took the struggle to the people, haranguing them personally. In one month, for example, he made thirty-four speeches that lasted up to six or seven hours each, cajoling, encouraging, demanding, instructing (Kinross, 1965, p. 416).

Finally, in 1926, the Treaty of Lausanne formalized the Turkish victory over their circumstances, and over the combined might of the Great War's winners. The Turks were masters of their own homeland, and gladly elected as their president the hero who had made it happen. Atatürk capitalized upon his window of opportunity to drive a comprehensive program of national reformation through the political apparatus.

A turning point in the conversion of the Turkish people from an empire dragging along a thousand years of tradition and history to a streamlined modern nation was the alphabet reform. Literacy skyrocketed, from 9% of the population in 1923 to 42% in 1938. However, the alphabet reform plus the "newspeak" language reform alienated the newly literate readers from the rest of the Muslim world, and from a written record that dated back to 800 AD. Morin discusses the nature of national memory, as analyzed by such scholars as Michel Foucault, and concludes that depriving the Turkish people of much of their history had political value. The Kemalists, the followers of Kemal Atatürk, controlled the past, and therefore, the future. The winners wrote the history books, and their version became canonized (Morin, 2004, pp. 55, 57).

In addition to the alphabet, Kemalist reforms displaced many entrenched customs, "teaching the people to write, read, speak, dress, think and live differently" (Morin, 2004, p. 59).

The "social reforms" that began in 1928 included sumptuary laws, surnames, and the Gregorian calendar. Turks discovered "the weekend" (Morin, 261). Atatürk "left nothing to chance" while forcing these cultural innovations through a cooperative legislature. Establishing a comprehensive system of state-funded and compulsory education also restrained the power of Islamic teachers by replacing, and suppressing, the traditional Islamic schools. This much change was too much for many traditional people to absorb. A number of violent uprisings were suppressed only by draconian "maintenance of order" laws, and by expanding the role of the army to guard against domestic enemies. Soldiers were, after all, the most respected professionals in their nation. Prior to the rise of Atatürk, the armed services included the most influential cadre of literate and educated men. Since his time, the military officer class has zealously guarded Atatürk's legacy, seeing themselves as the non-partisan "watchmen of the country," the honest umpires who blew the whistle on irresponsible politicians (Morin, 2004, pp. 260, 304, 285, 290, 298-299).

By late 1938, Kemal Atatürk had catalyzed the transformation of his people, and had no worlds left to conquer. More than 70 years later, Turks still remember the day, hour, and minute this "father and son of the nation" died. In a national ritual of formalized mourning, the Turks stop what they are doing every November 10 at 9:05 am to lower flags, blow car horns, and sound sirens. People stand for a minute of silence. School children take off the white collars of their uniforms and read poems about Atatürk's death, while wearing his icon on their chests (Morin, 2004, p. 20).

The Six Day Speech (Büyük Nutuk)

Nutuk, the Six Day Speech, is regarded in Turkey as a combination of the Mayflower Compact, Declaration of Independence, and Constitution – the document that defines their national identity (Morin, 2004, p. 20). It is also, as Davison writes, a document that has received too little scholarly attention in the Anglophone tradition of research (1998, p. 147).

Like Augustine's *City* and Calvin's *Institutes*, *Nutuk* took the enemies of the cause it espoused seriously, and sought to argue them off the public stage. Where Augustine frequently relied upon ridicule, as in his discussion concerning the deities of the wedding chamber (Augustine, 1961, p. 199), Atatürk marshaled the historical evidence, and allowed the telegrams composed at the time to argue his case for him.

Atatürk apparently won the argument. As a fresh interest in the political Islam of the Saudi-funded Wahabi sect stirs around the world (Gold, 2003), Turkish support for the ideology which supplanted official Islam in their nation can take the form of massive demonstrations in support of secularism. On April 29, 2007, more than a million demonstrators marched in İstanbul to protest the current government's perceived Islamic sympathies (Zambak, 2007). A fresh look at the document that still dominates the Turkish public imagination and national self-image is a timely research project.

Adak brought a feminist perspective to *Nutuk* studies by comparing this work to the memoirs of Atatürk's contemporary, a woman activist, Halide Edib (Adak, 2003). A 2004 dissertation by Aysel Morin provided an in-depth evaluation of *Nutuk* as an ideological work that used several "ideographs," short-hand symbols for expansive cultural themes. Other than these works, a literature search revealed no other scholarly articles published in the last decade.

Several factors may explain *Nutuk*'s current obscurity. Since its foundation, the Turkish Republic has kept a low profile. A policy of *Yurta sûlh, cihanda sûlh* (Peace at home, peace abroad) has kept the Turkish Republic out of other nations' wars and consequently out of the global news spotlight. For example, Turkey remained neutral for most of World War II, only declaring war on Japan in order to secure a place in the nascent United Nations (Lewis, 1960, p. 121).

A unique language barrier also needs to be considered. Even though modern Turkish is a fairly accessible language, with a Latinate orthography and a regular grammar, *Nutuk* was delivered in the courtly Turkish of the Ottoman era, a language now called "Osmanlı." A large percentage of the Osmanlı vocabulary was derived from Arabic and Persian sources. In a program described by sympathetic Turkish scholar Geoffrey Lewis as a "catastrophic success," the Atatürk regime embarked on "language reform." In an era of nationalistic exuberance, Atatürk's language reformers sought, or coined, "native" Turkish words to supplant the "foreign" words derived from Arabic and Persian. The "purified" language was a different language (G. Lewis, 2002).

This study relies upon three translations. An anonymously-translated English-language version was downloaded page by page from the internet. These 611 pages render *Nutuk* into 327,921 English words, in 6,910 paragraphs. Another English translation was published in 1985 in İstanbul. Both of these versions lack a table of contents and index. A modern Turkish translation, *Söylev*, published in 1997, contains a table of contents and index. It also bears evidence of condensation, since the text of the message occupies 383 pages in Söylev, as compared to 611 pages in the online English *Nutuk*, and 716 in the 1985 printed English *Nutuk*.

Nutuk begins with an introduction, a description of the early national meetings, and unflattering portraits of the functionaries surrounding the Sultan during the time of the Turkish War of Independence, the *Kurtuluş Savaşı* (Salvation Struggle). War stories balance the accounts of political and propaganda efforts. The Sultan is expelled, and the Caliphate, his religious office, abolished. Traditional dervish orders are suppressed as dangers to national peace and unity. *Nutuk* concludes with a rousing patriotic summons to the youth of Turkey to defend their sacred fatherland.

Until 2004, *Nutuk* had, as Davison wrote, received little attention in the Anglophone scholarly world (1998). Then, Aysel Morin published *Crafting A Nation: The Mythic Construction Of The New Turkish National Identity In Atatürk's Nutuk,* a landmark qualitative study of the central document of her own culture, her own nation.

With some caveats, Morin embraces the "modernization" theory of nation-formation. However, she argues that this theory places too much weight upon print capitalism by asserting that the medium is, itself, the primary message. Yes, it is necessary for a people to have a "shared text," a common "discourse." However, the role of the content of that text is slighted by the technological determinists. In order to understand the Turkish experience, Morin wrote, it is necessary to consider mythology, ideology, and rhetoric (2004, p. 32). We need to consider the "intimate interplay" of these factors, as well as the factors themselves, to properly understand Turkey, "the only democratic, secular, modern and pro-western Islamic nation." Somehow, the political rhetoric behind the Turkish identity sustains a paradoxical commitment to both modernity and to a collectivist, traditionalist, Islamic culture (Morin, 2004, pp. 3, 42).

Myths, she points out, especially cultural myths, typically are used as bridges, organizing time and events into a pattern, a shorthand. Atatürk, however, both used and dynamited this bridge. The cultural myths he selected bonded the Turks to their steppe-ranging noble ancestors, but broke with a thousand years of imperial Ottoman history (Morin, 2004, pp. 4, 28).

The myth of nationalism, which energized the secular governments taking shape in Europe, simultaneously undermined the Ottoman Empire and provided a transcendent rationale for Atatürk's new Turkish Republic (Morin, 2004, p. 14).

Dr. Morin's approach is to blend theories of myth and theories of nationalism in the crucible of communication research, in order to demonstrate how *Nutuk* used rhetoric to create "a people." The Turkish experience represents a unique test case, since their nationalistic evolution does not neatly fit into the existing scholarly paradigms (Morin, 2004, p. 27).

When Europe's economic, cultural, and industrial growth spurt began, the Ottoman Empire declined in prestige, and became, in the eyes of the West, a quaint "Arabian Nights" theme park, where men wore fezzes and kept harems. The real achievements of the Ottoman rulers, who deftly riding herd over a disparate assemblage of ethnic groups, including Persians, Arabs, and contentious European micro-nations, drifted out of focus (Morin, 2004, p. 45).

Morin vividly summarizes the Turkish conundrum:

> In his speeches, Atatürk re-defined the core of the Turkish national identity. He drew on age-old cultural constructs of Turks, melted their spirits in the industrial boilers of Kemalism on nationalist fire, and poured them into the clay pots of ancient cultures of Anatolia to create the "Turk," with a new Turkish identity based on (1) rejection of the Ottoman past and religious-based identity, (2) appropriation of the ancient Turkish cultural heritage, (3) westernization and (4) secularization. Accordingly, five main political myths emerged in the nationalist discourse to support the foundations of this new ideology: the Ancestor, First Duty,

Internal Enemy, Encirclement and Modem Europe. (2004, p. 60)

As Atatürk wrote *Nutuk,* groups of friends and coworkers gathered to hear the latest pages, commenting, debating, and enhancing the final project. One young participant in these symposiums wrote, "Atatürk used to get really excited while reading, as if he was reliving those days" (Morin, 2004, p. 75). The end product spanned a number of genres – speech, epic, history, personal memoir, and sermon (Morin, 2004, p. 77).

The myth of the first duty.

From the days of the earliest Turkish records, the Orkhon inscriptions, their national identity has been as a nation of soldiers. The Turkish man is socialized first by his family, then by his school, and finally by his mandatory term of military service. The formal Turkish word for soldier, *asker*, is matched by the informal *Mehmetçik*. This word combines Mehmet, the most common Turkish male name, with -çik, the affectionate diminutive suffix. Mehmetçik is ready to lay down his life for his nation, ready to, as the Turkish national anthem asserts, make his chest a shield for his country (Morin, 2004, pp. 93-94). When a busload of conscripts leaves a Turkish village, the smiling lads wave goodbye "with hennaed hands." This red dye has liturgical uses. It is applied to sheep that are ready to become dinner on the Feast of the Sacrifice (*Kurban Barami*), and to young brides ready to begin a new life (Anatolian, 2008).

This reverence for the military even extends to the enemy. When the monument to the fallen of Gallipolis was dedicated in 1934 Atatürk told the foreign guests:

> Those [Allied] heroes that shed their blood and lost their lives . . . you are now in the soil of a friendly country. Therefore rest in peace. There is no difference between the

Johnnies and the Mehmets to us when they lie side by side. You, the mothers who lost their sons from far away countries, wipe away your tears; your sons are now lying in our bosom and are in peace. After having lost their lives on this land, they have become our sons as well. (Meyer, 2003)

At the moment of the nation's greatest need, the avatar of the first duty appears: a credible hero with a record of successful military service, a man with a vision, with the clear call to duty, and with an extensive telegraph network (Morin, 2004, pp. 103, 115). The people are called to arms, summoned to defend their hearths and altars.

When facing a well-armed, well-organized invasion from Greek forces intent on reversing history's verdict against Byzantium, Atatürk's orders spoke of a "plain of defense:"

I said that there was no line of defence [*sic*] but a plain of defence, and that this plain was the whole of the country. Not an inch of the country should be abandoned until it was drenched with the blood of the citizens. Every unit, large or small, can be dislodged from its position, but every unit, large or small, re-establishes its front in face of the enemy at the first spot where it can hold its ground, and goes on fighting. Units which observe the neighbouring ones forced to retire must not link their own fate to theirs; they must hold their positions to the end. In this way every man of our troops obeyed this principle and fought step by step with the greatest devotion, and thus finally succeeded in crushing the superior hostile forces and deprived them of their power of attack and the possibility of continuing their offensive, and defeated them. (Atatürk, 458)

They fought. They endured. They prevailed. American novelist and eyewitness Ernest Hemingway saw, and was impressed. A rabble of demoralized veterans of a dirty, losing war was transformed into a victorious army. Their world would never be the same.

The myth of the internal enemy.

In the beginning of the Turkish War of Independence, Atatürk did not directly confront those he viewed as the larger Turkish problem, the Sultan and the government in İstanbul. Rather, he portrayed them as the captives and hostages of foreign powers. As the national drama developed, though, Atatürk's communications began sounding an additional theme, the Internal Enemy. Ever since the Orkhon inscriptions, the self-image of the Turks as invincible warriors drew upon this explanation for any reverses. Turks could only be defeated by other Turks, by those who failed to support their war chiefs (Morin, 2004, pp. 140-141). Internal enemies "embarrassed the ancestors by failing to perform their First Duty" (Morin, 2004, p. 143). Internal enemies came in two varieties: the short-sighted, and the corrupt. Some just wanted "peace in our time." Others hoped to profit, personally, from the reverses their nation suffered (Morin, 2004, p. 144). In a masterful propaganda coup, Atatürk pits one internal enemy (the Sultan) against another (the cabinet). He enlisted the allegiance of the Sultanate's supporters, even as he carefully arranged for that monarch's political downfall (Morin, 2004, pp. 158-160). As the Sultan defended his cabinet, Atatürk was able to portray the whole team as internal enemies of the real nation, thwarters of the national will, and degraded pawns of foreign powers (Morin, 2004, pp. 165-166).

The Sultan eventually left the country, harem in tow, for exile. As a sop to the religious groups, whose support was still needed, Atatürk permitted the election of a Caliph, a supreme Muslim religious leader. Atatürk bided his time, and waited for the new Caliph to overstep his bounds. It did not take long for Abdulmecit, the new Caliph, to start pontificating to the whole

Muslim world. At this point, "separation of mosque and state" becomes an iron-clad rule for the Turkish republic. The Internal Enemy paradigm placed the Caliph and his supporters on the wrong side of several schisms: "Republic versus Caliphate, progressives versus religious conservatives, Islam versus modern, revolutionaries (Kemalists) versus religious reactionaries" (Morin, 2004, p. 177).

When this process had run its course, an iron curtain was in place between modern Turkey and its Ottoman past (Morin, 2004, p. 183).

The myth of the ancestor.

The myth of the Ancestor required more careful handling. The pre-Islamic Turk was romanticized in the popular imagination as a valiant warrior, a lover of freedom, allergic to foreign yokes. On the other hand, though, he was usually at war, pursuing an aggressive, expansionist agenda. Atatürk calls upon his people to emulate their ancestor's historic virtues, and learn from their ancient mistakes:

> The political system which we regard as clear and fully realisable [*sic*] is national policy. In view of the general conditions obtaining in the world at present and the truths which in the course of centuries have rooted themselves in the minds of and have formed the characters of mankind, no greater mistake could be made than that of being a utopian. This is borne out in history and is the expression of science, reason and common sense.

> In order that our nation should be able to live a happy, strenuous and permanent life, it is necessary that the State should pursue an exclusively national policy and that this policy should be in perfect agreement with our internal organisation [*sic*] and be based on it. When I speak of national policy, I mean it in this sense: To work within our

national boundaries for the real happiness and welfare of the nation and the country by, above all, relying on our own strength in order to retain our existence. But not to lead the people to follow fictitious aims, of whatever nature, which could only bring them misfortune, and expect from the civilised [sic] world civilised human treatment, friendship based on mutuality. (Atatürk, 1985, p. 348)

Domineering empires belonged to the past. The future belonged to the ethnically compact nation, treating as an equal with other free nations in a spirit of civilized fraternity.

The myth of self-sufficiency.

A chronic theme in the Turkish epic is the need to be self-sufficient, since they could only depend on themselves. Atatürk used this Encirclement myth to demonize those who argued for making a negotiated settlement with the Entente powers. They were, he asserted, foolishly inviting the nation to politely place its head in a noose (Morin, 2004, p. 228).

The myth of modern Europe.

As he used the myth of Modern Europe, Atatürk appealed to the image of a shining new post-Christian, scientific Europe (Morin, 2004, p. 244). Atatürk's rhetoric concerning, and feelings toward, this Europe appear to be ambivalent. The European nations are models to be admired and emulated, and competitors to be resented. In order to catch up with these successful sibling nations, Turkey will need to follow their example and liberate the credulous, superstitious, priest-ridden peasants.

Atatürk drew heavily upon Ziya Gökalp's construct of separating the material and the cultural aspects of modernism, in order to suggest that a modern nation could indeed have a place for Islam, as long as it kept Islam in its place, as a private cultural adornment (Morin, 2004, p. 251). He also professed concern about those who would exploit religious sentiments for political gain (Morin, 2004, p. 253).

The "shared text" Atatürk left his nation aimed "to create a new and specific kind of loyalty from them," to enable the Turks to internalize their redefinition as modern citizens of a modern nation, the peer of all the other nations in the world (Morin, 2004, p. 277).

Some scholars distinguish between the "nation-state," such as Japan, which leans heavily on a shared tradition, and the "modern-state," such as the United States, which requires loyalty to a formal legal construct. Atatürk relied upon both binding valences to hold together the new republic he was giving his people (Morin, 2004, p. 280).

The myth of modern Europe gave the officers and gentlemen leading the Kemalist movement a standard to aspire to, and a platform from which they could look down upon the rustics and the hocas of village life (Morin, 2004, p. 305).

Consequences: A Secular Republic, a Muslim Society

Kemal Atatürk cited a traditional saying about his country and countrymen: *Biz bize benzeriz.* We resemble ourselves. Several factors in the Turkish heritage make their experience unique, fascinating, and worthy of more detailed study. Almost overnight, the Turkish people moved from being subjects of the Sultan/Caliph, the combined civic and religious leader of a polyglot empire, to citizens of a humanist republic. Atatürk, the undertaker of the old order and the midwife of the new, worked within the context of preexisting social and political trends. By the time he was finished, however, he led a people whose primary sense of corporate identity was rooted in the modern faith of nationalism, rather than in the traditional framing perspective of Islam.

In Dr. Morin's estimation, it took the peoples of Europe four centuries to make the transition from Christians to citizens. The Turkish Republic experienced a similar cultural transformation in ten years, from 1929 to 1939. The Turkish Republic is the epitome of the nationalist ideal. Unlike older orders that appealed to a transcendent source of validation, the nation of the nationalists claims to be its own *raison d'etre*. This is especially true for the new Turkish republic, which defined itself as the antithesis of the theocratic Islamic commonwealth it supplanted.

We will now examine several scholarly studies of nationalism, the religion that supplanted Islam as the heart of Turkish identity.

Nationalism.

The literature on nationalism and communication demonstrates how crucial a narrative is to the identity of a definable people. The "story" that has framed discourse in the west for more than 200 years is that of the State, described by Hegel as "places where providence manifests itself" (Dwyer, 2006). In practice, the national political order has offered a people a new collective identity to kill for, and to die for.

Anderson, imagined communities

The Sea of Faith

Was once, too, at the full, and round earth's shore

Lay like the folds of a bright girdle furled.

But now I only hear

Its melancholy, long, withdrawing roar,

Retreating, to the breath

Of the night-wind, down the vast edges drear

And naked shingles of the world.

("Dover Beach," Matthew Arnold)

Several new literary forms emerged at about the same time as the secular nation-state. As Anderson wrote, the nation and the newspaper, those children of "print capitalism," created a new way for people to share time together. The national newspaper became the new breviary, allowing millions to absorb the same stories, in the same official dialect, with their morning coffee (Bhabha, 1990, p. 49). Novels, too, shaped the shared national conversation. Miguel de Cervantes lampooned the departing feudal order, even as Daniel DeFoe's marooned islander brought Protestant civilization to his new territory.

"Man shall not live by bread alone," Jesus told his adversary in a famous confrontation (Matt. 4:4). The 900 worshippers at Jonestown chose death over the loss of the religious community that gave meaning to their lives. In the aftermath of the Protestant Reformation, people of faith killed and died for their faith. As men who bore the name of Christian perpetrated atrocities upon one another, the growing skepticism toward all religious faith left a vacuum. The "imagined community," the nation, arose to fill this need. Once again, citizens, like saints, had something bigger than themselves to belong to, something that could outlive them, something worth dying to protect (Anderson, 1991, p. 7; Bhabha, 1990, p. 19).

Several social and technological developments combined to make the nation model "modular," portable to other climes and contexts. The most important of these was "print capitalism," as expressed in the newspaper and the novel. This development had an impact on the relative importance of various languages (Bhabha, 1990, p. 48-52).

During the pre-modern era, sacred languages created unified communities of faith across diverse cultures. Church Latin tied together western Christendom, Greek served the needs of the Byzantine court, and Arabic prayers traveled with Sinbad around much of the globe (Anderson, 1991, pp. 15-22; Pei, 1965, p. 208). The court language of the Ottoman Empire, Ottoman Turkish (*Osmanlı*), grafted poetic vocabularies from Persian and judicial vocabularies from Arabic onto a Turkish skeleton. The ideograms of written Chinese united an empire with hundreds of mutually unintelligible dialects (Pei, 1965, p. 92).

Before 1500, perhaps 77% of books printed were in Latin. Then, between 1518 and 1525, a third of all the books published in the German language came from the pen of Martin Luther (Anderson, 1991, p. 39). Along with independent nations and national churches, vernacular was on the rise. Every self-respecting nation needed its own national language.

Novels, newspapers, and dictionaries served to establish official national languages in the 18th century. Daniel DeFoe published political newspapers and wrote *Robinson Crusoe*. Parisian French became the standardized language of Republican France, with its own linguistics institute to keep *notre langue propre* properly managed. Meanwhile, in the provinces, the local patois survived (Merle, 1975). Official German was the language of novelists, poets, and journalists. Regional dialects were the language of everyday life. Alessandro Manzoni's *I Promessi Sposi* and Collodi's *Pinocchio* celebrated vernacular, secular, national Italian language and life (Manzoni, 1967; Collodi, 1983).

One reason why the Ottoman Empire found itself behind the West was the earlier embrace in Europe of print technology. The first printing press set up in the Ottoman Empire began operating nearly 300 years after Gutenberg modified a wine press. This hindered education and industrialization. As a further blow to print culture, non-print technologies, such as the telegraph and radio, made it possible to jump directly from the oral stage of cultural transmission to the electronic era. Today, most printing is done for schools. An average of one daily newspaper rolls off the presses for every 15 Turks (Morin, 2004, pp. 282-283).

The clerics of the new collective entities, the nations, consisted of "internal pilgrims" who followed their ambitions away from diverse neighborhoods to universities in capitol cities. Here, they were immersed in the nation's administrative language, and eventually sent to staff bureaucracies throughout the nation. They frequently had more in common with one another than they did with the kin and neighbors they had left behind (Anderson, 1991, p. 115).

Modern schools offered to transform the lives of students. The local schoolmaster was often an "internal pilgrim" from another part of the nation, motivated by a desire to bring enlightenment to the benighted rustics. The sadistic Welsh schoolmaster in the novel *How Green Was My Valley*, ashamed of his mother tongue and determined to anglicize his students, apparently is modeled on real exemplars (Llewellyn, 1997, p. 202). The value of public schooling is also one of the primary themes of Pinocchio. Carlo Lorenzini, better known by his pen name Collodi, was a professional educator whose most famous "lecture" appeared week after week in a newspaper column about a marionette that came to life (Collodi, 1983).

The peripatetic bureaucrat, the agent of the central government, the apostle of the new nation, frequently did the heavy lifting required to re-envision and re-define his society. Census takers established formal social strata. Maps created instant logos for nationalist movements, as well as visual indicators of historical trends. Military officers absorbed quaint courtliness, and skill in modern weapons, from the

Western powers. As an organized and armed body, the Turkish military played a significant role in both the Tanzimat and the Young Turk movements. This was also the nursery of Atatürk's career (Morin, 2004, p. 304).

Nation and Narration.

Nation and Narration, an anthology collected by Homi K. Bhabha, brings together a few more reflections on the intertwining natures of national and literary consciousness.

Renan wrote of how the Turkish identity was diluted by the Ottoman Empire, which insisted on bringing disparate people and national traditions under its aegis. "Each defeat advanced the cause of Italy; each victory speed doom for Turkey; for Italy is a nation, and Turkey, outside of Asia Minor, is not one." Renan views national consciousness as a shared legacy of things a group of people remember, and things they feel compelled to forget. As a Frenchman, he glories in the fact that his people "founded the principle of nationality" in 1789, by anchoring its common identity in a set of propositions rather than in a religious creed (Bhabha, 1990, p. 12).

Martin Thom's essay, "Tribes within Nations," considers how a primary activity of the nation-building process, at least in the French experience, was suppressing the influence of local religious authorities. A major tool for this eradication of past, prior, parochial allegiances was "universal, free, lay, primary education" (Bhabha, 1990, p. 20).

Timothy Brenan's essay "The National Longing for Form" describes the nation as an entity imbued with numinous transcendence by the stories it generates. Epics yield to novels, religious rituals to political rites. Much new literature, interestingly enough, mines the mother lode of traditional peasant culture in order to adorn the new cosmopolitan national identity (Bhabha, 1990, p. 53).

In a sense, then, nationalist doctrine takes over religion's social role, and substitutes for the imperial church. The most successful early European nationalist was Napoleon, who decried the regal centralization of power while marching across Europe in the name of Republican France. In its European origins, nationalism was frankly messianic. According to Kohn, modern nationalism took three concepts from Old Testament mythology: "the idea of a chosen people, the emphasis on a common stock of memory of the past and hopes for the future, and finally national messianism" (Bhabha, 1990, p. 59).

In the concluding article in this collection, Bhabha agrees. "The nation fills the void left in the uprooting of communities and kin, and turns that loss into the language of metaphor" (Bhabha, 1990, p. 291).

With deed and word, Atatürk was able to persuade a nation to downplay its Islamic identity, and embrace nationalism as the new way of defining themselves as a corporate entity.

Current status of Islam in Turkey.

Despite an official secular governmental structure, or perhaps because of it, the Turkish people remain deeply committed to their Muslim faith. Yet even the religious clerics and people operate within the frame of reference Atatürk established. Laicism (*laiklik*) does not mean the suppression of religion, but its domestication. Religious people and resources, in a laicized society, are under the oversight and control of non-religious people and institutions. We will consider the ongoing vitality of Islamic popular culture in the Turkish Republic of today, as it carefully negotiates a rapprochement with the officially and militantly secular culture of public life. We will also consider the insights of Nobel prize-winning Turkish novelist Orhan Pamuk concerning the Turkish view of the West.

Andrew Davison's book *Secularism and Revivalism in Turkey: A Hermeneutic Reconsideration* uses the "hermeneutic" perspective of Hans-Georg Gadamer to examine the ideological environment of present-day Turkey. In order to understand what motivates people from a completely different culture, we need to start by "foregrounding" our own prejudices, Gadamer wrote. No scholar can hope to divorce himself from his own culture. He can, however, be aware of the influences that color his observations, make allowances for them, and thereby achieve more accuracy in describing the inner world of other cultures (Davison, 1998, p. 5).

The Turkish Republic, Davison writes, is significant because of its location on several boundaries.

> Taking place on the geographic edge of the Islamic world and Europe, between East and West, the dialogue over the meanings and ends of secularization and modernization since the founding of the laicist republic in the 1920s has had world historical significance both for Turks and for interpreters of Turkey. (1998, p. 9)

Gadamer took the position that the "secular Weltanschauung" of most social science blinds its practitioners to the forces that move most of the world (Davison, 1998, p. 26). Secularists assume that time is an arrow, a one-way progression away from traditional worlds to modernism. New loyalties, to nation-states, replace old allegiances to clan and church (Davison, 1998, p. 39).

Most social scientists, apart from the hermeneutic camp, insist on "non-interpretive" methodologies, especially when dealing with other cultures. The apparent success of the Turkish republic in displacing a traditional order with a self-consciously "scientific" society has, Davison wrote, "made Turkey a site of great interest for modern political scientists" (1998, p. 87).

Much of Davison's book deals with Atatürk's mentor, Ziyan Gökalp. A follower of Emile Durkheim, Gökalp believed that history was propelled by big ideas, "collective representations." To truly join the modern world, Gökalp wrote, it was necessary to re-adjust the relationships between Islam and the other partners in the creation of culture: Turkish nationalism and modernity. In Gökalp's envisioned new order, Islam was quite the junior partner, a family heirloom worth retaining for its cultural heritage and for the social cement this common set of values provided (Davison, 1998, pp. 102, 111). The Turkish national identity, however, owed far more to linguistic and cultural factors than it did to Islam (Davison, 1998, p. 112). Gökalp made a distinction between formal "civilization," the "rational concepts of a nation," and the informal "culture" enjoyed by people in their private lives.

When Gökalp's protégé, Atatürk, began to implement this laicising program, he stepped into the longstanding subjugation of religious life to the interests of the state. The goal was to assert lay control over religious leaders and their message (Davison, 1998, p. 140). There was a difference, though. This time, the state was not claiming to act in the interests of global Islam, but only in its own interests.

Davison notes the research of Şerif Mardin, who discussed the conflicts between the traditional Turkish culture and the positivism that underlay the assurance of Atatürk and his coterie. Materialistic positivism allowed these shapers of the new Turkey to preen themselves on their superior mental prowess (Davison, 1998, p. 155).

However, their hypertrophied brains were gained, Mardin suggested, at the expense of their overall humanity:

> Depriving a person of his ability to use the set of symbols which shape his individual approach to God may be a more distressing blow to him than depriving him of other values. It may be easier to take defeat on the battlefield than to be deprived of the means of personal access to the sacred, especially if this access is one of the processes that make for mental equilibrium, personal satisfaction, and integration with the rest of society." (cited in Davison, 1998, p. 155)

Or, as Christian commentator C. S. Lewis suggested, perhaps the heads of skeptical secularists look bigger, since their chests have atrophied (1974, p. 25).

The separation of Islam from life happened at a number of levels. For example, the Kemalists spoke of "protecting" religion from the rough-and-tumble of public life, while letting it have free reign over the individual conscience. Each time *laiklik* is advocated, though, the goal is to more closely approach the "civilized" condition of secular Europe (Davison, 1998, p. 161).

The formal laicization of Turkish society came in two stages. The 1921 constitution dismissed the Caliph, but maintained that Islam was still the state religion. The 1928 constitution eliminated even that token recognition (Davison, 1998, p. 162).

A key element to breaking the hold of religious authority, and religious authorities, over public life was state control over education. Although Sultan Abdul Hamid II had tried to fill the new wineskins of modern, European-style schools with the fine aged wine of religious faith, the Kemalist revolution viewed their schools as the means for advancing "progress," and inculcating a secular, scientific perspective in their future citizens. National success, the Atatürk coterie believed, depended on the strict separation of religion and education, of faith and reason. Islam, Atatürk believed, engendered fatalism, passivity, and lethargy (Davison, 1998, p. 164). The Kemalist modernization project was, in the memories of that generation of students, the "children of the revolution," an amazing new epoch in history, a new social order breaking in with new possibilities and unlimited horizons (Özyürek, 2006, pp. 29-30).

The policies of the Republican People's Party, the vehicle of Atatürk's political career, "have been viewed as fundamental in advancing Turkey's maturity from one civilization (old, traditional, fatalist, and dominated by Islam) to another (New, modern, active, and dominated by science)" (Davison, 1998, p. 176).

Turkish scholar E. Fuat Keyman borrows John Thompson's paradigm to assert that a culture can use a tradition in several different ways: as a tool for interpreting life today, as a set of norms, as an identity, and for legitimation. *Kemalism*, adherence to the values of Kemal Atatürk, Keyman writes, can be effectively employed as a hermeneutic. Kemalism works to support an organic view of society, where politics seeks the common good, under the guidance of an elite that is motivated by the "will to civilization." Kemalism also defines the nation's state as the "active and sovereign subject of civilization." The citizens are soldiers in the march of progress, "objects and bearers of the will to civilization." *"Kemalist modernite projesi Platoncudur; aynı mantık içinde, 'toplumsal yarar' nosyonuyla toplumsal talepler arasın kesin bir çizgi çizererk . . ."* Keyman wrote, describing the use Kemal Atatürk made of "modernism" as a platonic ideal, a clear-cut path to that which is decisively best for the nation (Keyman, 1997).

In an essay on *autonomization*, another Turkish scholar, Nilüfer Göle, attempts to recast the ongoing oscillations between secular elites and popular religious figures as a discussion, not between progress and reaction or science and superstition, but as a dialogue between two different kinds of modernization. The "modernizing" elites, characterized by an antipathy toward religious influence, are being displaced by the "technocratic elites," who wish to have the best of both worlds, and fold Islamic values into a pragmatic program. The technocratic elites began gaining influence in the 1980s with their "quest for consensus," and willingness to dialogue with Islamic leaders. The rise of these "Islamic engineers" signaled the end of the old-fashioned modernizing era – that earlier Republican era which sought to build utopia from scratch, adopting a *tabula rasa* perspective. This "single-actor syndrome" that viewed the state, the political order, as the only creative force in society, led to "the hypertrophied statism of the 1970s."

This statism raised the stakes, and the tensions, between the official leadership and those who spoke out for the aspirations of the pious people. Much of the conflict can be ascribed to contrasting idealisms. The "past utopians" of the political right looked back on the early days of the Turkish Republic with a paralyzing nostalgia, while the "future utopians" of the left looked forward to how great things could be. Both imaginative perspectives froze out discourse with the present reality. European liberalism celebrates the rise of the individual. Turkish liberalism celebrates the rise of the non-state center as the economic dimension of autonomization. In the Turkish milieu, liberalism does not mean individualism, but the rise of non-state actors. Islam still governs the cultural dimension of Turkish life on an informal level, and seeks to speak aloud the values that had been confined to private life for several generations (Göle, 1994).

Carol Delaney's *Father State, Mother Land* brings the perspective of gender studies to the conversation. Nationalism is, she points out, entwined with religion, kin, and politics. She cites Anderson's description of the "conceptual similarity" – all of these social groups seek corporate unity (1995).

The Turkish *aile* (family) consists of the wife and children. It is something a man has. "Father state epitomized Ottoman rule," Delaney writes, while Atatürk's rhetorical strategy "reconfigured the imaginative terrain as he sought to redefine the physical." The deeply embedded allegiance to motherhood in Turkish culture was directed toward the nation, even as the Turkish women were emancipated to be more than mothers, to participate fully in public and civic life (Delaney, 1995).

Reşat Kasaba uses Marshal Berman's paradigm of modernization as "generalized images which summarize the various transformations of social life" that pace the growth of the market society and nation-state. As the "public sphere" increases in power and allure, traditional kinship and family bonds attenuate. The State becomes the ground of social and personal reality. One factor, Kasaba asserts, that made Turkey the poster child for modernization is that the military and political elite who drove the program had time to sweep the inconsistencies under the rug before western social scientists started taking notice. They made the process look "streamlined and unilinear." One such scholar, Bernard Lewis, viewed *The Emergence of Modern Turkey* (B. Lewis, 1968) through the lens of this "trans-historical strait jacket." Lewis asserted that the Turks made two good choices during the course of their long history. During the middle ages, they moved from Asia toward Europe. Then, in the 1920s, they turned their backs on politicized Islam to build a secular nation (Kasaba, 2000).

Kasaba's description of "Turkish modernization and the modernizing elite" stresses the top-down nature of the Kemalist revolution. Like the French Jacobins, the Turkish Republicans viewed their nation as a project to impose upon an inert people "for their own good." The modernizers viewed modernism, per se, as a numinous entity, a god-substitute. Now, progress was God, and the stock market would go up forever.

The Ottoman Turks were, Atatürk asserted, blindsided by the modern world because their minds were entirely too medieval – rigid, inflexible, backwards. "We lived through pain," he said. And civilization was not kind, not forgiving. In words of demagogic urgency familiar to the politician's lexicon Atatürk said, "We have to move forward. Civilization is such a fire that it burns and destroys those who ignore it" (Kasaba, 2000).

The new identity Atatürk imposed upon his nation – a Turkish people living in a Turkish homeland, speaking an updated, streamlined Turkish language, under the aegis of a modern, but home-grown, Turkish state – alienated two groups. There was no room in the public sphere of this new world for Islamists, even intellectual, thoughtful, and popular Islamic leaders. And life became very hard for ethnic minorities. The Armenians were ushered out of the picture before Atatürk came to power. Greek and Turkish populations were "exchanged" in several stages, before and after the Turkish War of Independence, as national boundaries settled down. The most significant exile, however, was imposed by the tutelary elite upon themselves, as they attempted to enforce a new "year zero" that repudiated the Ottoman order that had held sway over much of the globe for more than five centuries (Gülalp, 2005).

Perhaps, Gülalp hopes, the kinder and gentler aspects of the modernizing project – concern for human and civil rights, the reliance upon market forces to regulate human intercourse rather than brute force or thoughtless tradition – will result in a world less hard-edged than the pitilessly rectilinear vision of the Kemalist could imagine (Gülalp, 2005). Of course, much depends upon the next moves of the European Union, the new Mecca of the modernizing elite. The continuing foot-dragging that attends Turkey's suit for full inclusion is made all the more painful by the ease with which former Soviet-bloc nations leaped to the front of the queue.

> Having rejected Mecca, and then being rejected by Brussels, where does Turkey look? Tashkent may be the answer. The end of the Soviet Union gives Turkey the opportunity to become the leader of a revived Turkic civilization involving seven countries from the borders of Greece to those of China. (Huntington, 1993)

Roberts ascribed this war of paradigms to Western meddling. Muslim extremists arose after decades of Western colonization and secularization that has created a *modern* elite, Muslim in name only, to rule over religious people and to suppress Islamic mores. All experts "know" this, and most of them hail it as bringing progress and development to the Muslim world (Roberts, 2009).

What do the Turks themselves have to say in Turkish-language scholarly journals? Three representative articles were reviewed. The Kasaba article had an English summary, but yielded additional nuances when read in Turkish. The other two articles were translated, summarized, and paraphrased by this writer, with the assistance of a native speaker. These scholars demonstrate the ongoing ambivalence toward the Kemalist legacy.

Bayram Kodaman's 1998 article *Atatük'un Milli Birlik ve Milli Devlet Anlayışı* (*Atatürk's Insights into National Unity and National*

Government) is worth translating and summarizing at some length. Kodaman speaks of two national awakenings, which culminated in 1923, when Atatürk created a new national identity from the material of the preexisting Ottoman Empire, even as the Ottoman Empire evolved from the earlier Selçuk Empire. The Ottomans were bound together by a political dynasty, a religious dynasty, and a tribal unity based on a common understanding. However, they were also a cosmopolitan people, who lived with a sense of conflict, of double-mindedness. Atatürk knew this very well, and set about transforming the defining condition of his people into an allegiance to a national government. This was his most challenging task. He tried to utilize their existing sense of unity in their identity as Ottomans, their residual loyalty to state and country. But it was necessary to create one new national consciousness. Within the clear borders of a national state, he sought to create one state, based on a national consciousness rooted in Turkish language and culture. This method and analysis rejects racism, parochialism, sectarianism, and *kavmiyetcilik*, or old religion. Perhaps "fundamentalism" would accurately capture the sense of this word. The goal pursued by this approach was to create an educated society. Accordingly, in 1924 Atatürk moved to reform and unify education, to make sure that Turks shared a common education, culture, and civilization. To achieve national unity, it was necessary to displace both primitive local dialects and the baroque, ornate, courtly Osmanlı with a "civilized" language, a modern Anatolian Turkish. The aim of language reform was to provide the Turks with a common language. The conclusion Kodaman reached was:

> *Türk devletinin milli ve laik yapısı kesinlikle değiştirilmemelidir. Aksi halde devleti ve toplumu huzura kavuşturmak imkansızdır. Türk devlet modeli, diğer türk develetlerine ve İslam devletlerine model olma özelliğini devam ettirmelidir.*

The Turkish national government and laicist order can absolutely never be changed. Otherwise, it is impossible to establish or restore governmental or social peace. The Turkish model of government must maintain the essential nature of its model of government in the face of models chosen by other Turkic or Islamic States. (Kodaman, 1998; trans. Smedley)

Resat Kasaba's discussion of the conflict between *Kemalist Certainties and Modern Ambiguities* focuses on the fault lines appearing in what had seemed, to outside eyes, a monolithic social consensus. Rather than a homogenous modern state, the Turks precipitated into contrasting layers – "Muslim and secularist, Turk and Kurd, reason and faith, rural and urban – in short, the old and the new" (2000).

Many of the underlying conflicts began to emerge in the 1980s, as religious parties sought a more assertive role in public life, while the "tutelary elite," the armed forces who viewed themselves as the guardians of the Kemalist legacy, exerted undue influence on the political process from time to time. The secular elite had an explanation for the continuing national social, economic, and political disappointments: the backward, regressive, *religious* elements were obviously sabotaging the "linear" trajectory toward modern wealth, abundance, and international respect. Push the Islamic genii back into its bottle, and progress could resume. Democracy was fine, as long as it didn't vote the wrong kind of people into power.

The religious parties, on the other hand, pointed out that the secularists had enjoyed more than half a century of a free hand at managing the nation's affairs, with disappointing results. Therefore, maybe it was time to try something else.

Meanwhile, as the secularists with their military bodyguards confronted the religious parties with their popular support, the Kurdish nationalists poured a little more gasoline on the flames of civic unrest. The Kurds are, after all, the largest linguistic community in the world without a nation of their own, since their people are distributed over parts of Turkey, Iran, Iraq, and Afghanistan. Three hostile absolutist groups confront each other, each convinced of its sole claim to truth.

Perhaps, Kasaba suggests, all three parties need to step back from the edge of the abyss, take a deep breath, and foreswear their claims to corner the market for truth. A little ambiguity, a healthy dose of tolerance, and the Turks should be able to muddle through to a conclusion everyone finds acceptable:

> I take the skepticism of recent years as an opportunity to question the suprahistorical pretensions of all absolutist ideologies. I seek to recapture some of the early indeterminate richness of Ottoman and Turkish modernization by taking it out of the iron-clad pathways into which it was forced in subsequent years. (Kasaba, 2000)

Meanwhile, the cult of Atatürk has deep roots in the national identity. This is not universally celebrated. The article *Atatürk ve Atatürkçuler* (Kabaklı, 1998) asserts that the religious fervor displayed by the Atatürk loyalists goes over the edge, into idolatry – *putperestlik* – a word that triggers visceral revulsion for any observant Muslim. *Atatürk'ün gerçeğini bulmalıyız,* wrote Turkish scholar Ahmet Kabaklı: "We must find the truth about Atatürk" (1998). This is a difficult project, he asserts, because of all the vested interests that have a stake in maintaining the cult of Atatürk. Granted, *en kara günlerde*, during the darkest days of the Turkish national story, Atatürk earned the eternal gratitude of his people by rescuing their national existence. This virtuous achievement cannot be denied, despite the hero's errors, faults, and mistakes. Since then, however, insincere people have used a false press, lying books, and pretentious artifices for their personal advantage. Kabaklı views this as a despicable idolatry, a terrifying apotheosis of a mere human. The toadies, the bootlickers, use Atatürk's guiding words – revolutionary, reformist, progressive – to adorn their hard-core, fanatical stupidity. These kinds of people are a resented, ongoing trial to Kabaklı. The cult of Atatürk, he complains, resembles the worst excesses of Christian piety, especially the Catholic variety with its elaborate hierarchs and pompous formalities (1998).

"Godwin's Law," an aphorism current among those who participate in online debates, holds that the first person to invoke the name of Hitler ends the conversation and loses the argument. In the context of Turkish discourse, Kabaklı writes, anyone who wants to end dialogue needs only to malign his opponent as "an enemy of Atatürk" – *Atatürk düşmanı!* The bottom line, Kabaklı asserts, is that the Turkish people have an enduring destiny of their own. They are not mere appendages to Kemal Atatürk, and the book of their history is more than just an appendix to the Great Man's biography (1998).

Perhaps the best summary of the current condition of the Kemalist legacy available in English is Esra Özyürek's book-length dissertation *Nostalgia for the Modern: State Secularism and Everyday Politics in Turkey*. The Turkish public square is slowly being emptied of its governing icon, as "The Elderly Children of the Republic" die off, and take with them their memories of how Atatürk's regime was perceived as the beginning of a whole new world, the intrusion of a fresh, modern, scientific, and salvific social order (Özyürek, 2006, p. 29). Atatürk himself is miniaturized, as his intimidating image is domesticated. Traditional portraits, bust only, dominate viewers by glaring directly at them from the wall in every classroom, every public office (Morin, 2004, p. 19). The kinder, gentler Atatürk is portrayed in social settings, looking at the others in the picture, rather than staring out of the picture at the viewer. He is no longer the floating head of the body politic, but a man among men. Although there is still a robust market for Atatürk hagiography and iconography, the more personable, privatized images are growing in popularity (Özyürek, 2006, p. 116).

School children may still memorize hundreds of Atatürk aphorisms as guides to conduct, and loudly recite nationalist poems (*Atatürk ölmedi yüreğimde yaşıyor* – Atatürk didn't die, he lives within my heart …) (Özyürek, 2006, p. 132), but the Islamist parties remember history differently. Crowds of women with head scarves and men with beards gather to remember the state of flux that prevailed in the early days of the Republic, when Muslim leaders were assiduously courted, and their help enlisted, in the rebuilding of a shattered people (Özyürek, 2006, p. 165). They recall how the first constitution of the Turkish Republic bluntly stated that "Islam is the state religion." As George Orwell's *1984* suggested, those who control the past control the present (1977, p. 35). In contemporary Turkey, "public memory" is a "political battleground" (Özyürek, 2006, p. 151). Yet both forms of nostalgia, Islamic and secular, are emblematic of a loss of hope toward the future.

How shall we then live?

"You can't fight something with nothing," an American political aphorism holds. Those who wish to build upon, or to replace, Atatürk's legacy would do well to consider the structural elements of his vision, the components that meshed with human needs so well that the social order he catalyzed endured as well as it did, and for as long as it did. Social orders can, and do, decay. Fragile worlds do need to be maintained.

Broken worlds must be repaired. The need for diagnostic and repair manuals sometimes becomes acute. Those who would write such documents would do well to study models that actually worked.

In Chapter 3, we will use the paradigm of "the treaty of the great king," first expounded by Meredith Kline and later extended by other Calvinist scholars, to survey the shared themes of *Nutuk* and the *City of God*, the emphases that hint at explanations for the source of their rhetorical and historical power.

In Chapter 4, we will examine Atatürk's *Nutuk* using open-source software to compare its themes to those in Augustine's *City of God*, and to isolate the persuasive elements they share. Since *City of God* has already been studied extensively, we will use it in that chapter as a *tool* of analysis, rather than as a *subject* of analysis. It is our "gold standard" of a document that catalyzed the social construction of a new reality, when a powerful social order suddenly lost its credibility.

Biz bize benziriz, Atatürk once famously remarked, when describing the Turks. "We resemble ourselves." The software provides a list of nearly 200 words that occur with matching frequency in these two documents. Since these terms already match, they will by definition have a correlation of 1. In order to aggregate the shared terms into more useful summaries, we will need to bring an additional yardstick to the workbench. We selected Plato's *Republic* as our "iron pyrite standard," assuming that the intensity with which Augustine and Atatürk disagree with Plato will clarify the areas where they agree with each other.

Finally, in Chapter 5, we will discuss the implications of the themes highlighted by our qualitative and quantitative analyses.

Chapter 3: A Qualitative Comparison

In earlier chapters, we have examined a fascinating class of events, a "what." In two widely contrasting contexts, a collapsing empire was replaced by something that was, arguably, a more human, and humane, social order. Atatürk and Augustine both managed to create a credible alternate vision for how life could be structured, and lived.

The research question to be now considered is "how." What rhetorical strategies did both men employ to reshape hopes, dreams, and expectations? Perhaps, both leaders provided believable answers to the handful of basic questions that underlie any viable social order.

A Useful Paradigm: The Suzerainty Treaty

Several millennia before Atatürk, another military leader and statesman climaxed his career by addressing his people with one final oration, spread out over several days. With language that was in turns legalistic and lyrical, Moses summed up for Israel the events that had brought them to this point in their history, and the requirements that the new life they were about to enter would impose upon them. The Book of Deuteronomy impressed the inspired vision of Moses upon Israel, providing explanations that were cited in future challenges, such as three sneering questions addressed to the epitome of Israel at the beginning of his public ministry (Matthew 4; Luke 4). The patterns of power and persuasion employed by Moses still provide insights today's researcher can find profitable.

The task at hand is to find, and describe, common themes in two world-changing documents. Given a plethora of complex data, what meta-pattern will simplify matters, help to clarify things, bring order out of chaos, and draw meaning out of confusion? Many frames of reference, or systems of interpretation, could be applied. For the purposes of this study, a paradigm that first appeared in the essays of Biblical scholar Meredith Kline looks useful. Again, the issue is the definition of a social order. Kline proposed a succinct way to do exactly that. In his book *The Treaty of the Great King* Kline analyzed the book of Deuteronomy in terms of its cultural and historic setting, and suggested that it was modeled on the suzerainty treaty of its day. YWYH, as the Great King, treats with Israel, as the subject people, specifying expectations and requirements on the parts of both parties. A functional treaty defined the social reality of the subject people, and specified a handful of irreducible criteria. Kline summarized these, in one of his essays, as:

I. Preamble: Covenant Mediator, 1:1-5

II. Historical Prologue: Covenant History, 1:6-4:49

III. Stipulations: Covenant Life, 5:1-26:19

IV. Sanctions: Covenant Ratification, 27:1-30:20

V. Dynastic Disposition: Covenant Continuity, 31:1-34:12

Someone needs to make the covenant, and to explain the reasons why, at a specific point in history, a new social order needs to be welcomed and embraced. The covenant maker, treaty imposer, or suzerain needs to lay out his expectations for the behavior of the subject people, demand their participation, and spell out the consequences of violating the covenant. Finally, the suzerain needs to make it clear how the new social arrangement will be propagated. He needs to describe the mechanisms for succession planning.

Kline's paradigm was developed and applied in a variety of contexts by other Calvinist scholars and writers. Ray Sutton absorbed the various ways that Kline presented the components of the covenant, then applied the paradigm to the books of Deuteronomy, Psalms, and Matthew, all of which broke down into five logical segments. When he shared these insights with a study group, another member, David Chilton, discovered that this same pattern brought cohesion and clarity to his in-progress exposition of the book of Revelation.

The fine-tuned version of the five-point covenant model that emerged from this circle of scholars, which grew to include George Grant and Gary North, can be summarized thus:

1. Transcendence
2. Hierarchy / Authority
3. Ethics
4. Oath / Judgment / Sanctions
5. Succession / Continuity / Inheritance

This study argues that, since Augustine and Atatürk both provided intellectually and emotionally satisfying answers to all five questions, their visionary works had both immediate credibility and generation-spanning relevance. To launch and maintain a new order, visionaries need to be able to tell their followers:

1. Who is in charge here?
2. To whom do I report?
3. What are the rules?
4. What happens if I obey / disobey?
5. Does this outfit have a future? (DeMar, p. xiv)

How do these principles apply to the documents at hand?

The First Principle: Transcendence/Historical Prologue

A new world has arrived. But where did it come from? And how did it get here?

A new reality requires a new validation, a new transcendent justification. This includes fresh values to embrace, and revised evils to revile. Kurt Gödel's incompleteness theorem demonstrates that no system of rule-based reasoning can be understood in terms of its own frame of reference (Hofstadter, 1979). This is true of social orders as well as of mathematical systems. Unless a society points to something beyond itself, it has no transcendent reason to exist. The stark Soviet-era Georgian film *Repentance* is framed by vignettes, before and after the main action of the film, of gossiping shopkeepers. In the first brief scene, they take note of an old woman approaching. In the final scene, the passerby leans on her cane and asks for directions to a church.

"There is no church on Varlam Street," the shopkeepers explain.

"What is the point of a road that does not lead to a church?" she retorts, then hobbles off (Abuladze, 1986).

A moment of transcendence is a moment of transition. Kline's *historical prologue* speaks of a decision point. The old order is dead. The new order has arrived. The doomed empire might strike back, but in vain; a new hope appears. The successful world-changing message has both negative and positive elements; a devil and a deity; something slimy to shun, something shining to embrace.

How, then, did Atatürk and Augustine's messages incorporate the transcendent element every significant document needs?

Atatürk and the first theme.

The Book of Deuteronomy presents Moses as a sage, a leader, bequeathing his nation a retrospective glance at the trials, traumas, struggles, and victories that brought them to this point in their history. In Nutuk, Kemal Atatürk did the same.

His nation had met, and defeated, the greatest threat they ever faced to their existence. A millennium of unbroken victories, followed by several centuries of contraction, climaxed in a final attempt to obliterate the Turkish national identity. In the stirring words that open this epic speech, Atatürk hints at the devil of his cosmology, and makes it plain where the shame, blame, and opprobrium rest:

Gentlemen,

I landed at Samsoon on the 19th May, 1919. This was the position at that time:

The group of Powers which included the Ottoman Government had been defeated in the Great War. The Ottoman Army had been crushed on every front. An armistice had been signed under severe conditions. The prolongation of the Great War had left the people exhausted and impoverished. Those who had driven the people and the country into the general conflict had fled and now cared for nothing but their own safety. Wahideddin, the degenerate occupant of the throne and the Caliphate, was seeking for some despicable way to save his person and his throne, the only objects of his anxiety. The Cabinet, of which Damad Ferid Pasha was the head, was weak and lacked dignity and courage. It was subservient to the will of the Sultan alone and agreed to every proposal that could protect its members and their sovereign.

The Army had been deprived of their arms and ammunition, and this state of affairs continued.

The Entente Powers did not consider it necessary to respect the terms of the armistice. On various pretexts, their men-of-war and troops remained at Constantinople. The Vilayet of Adana was occupied by the French; Urfah, Marash, Aintab, by the English. In Adalia and Konia were the

Italians, whilst at Merifun and Samsoon were English troops. Foreign officers and officials and their special agents were very active in all directions. At last, on the 15th May, that is to say, four days before the following account of events begins, the Greek Army, with the consent of the Entente Powers, had landed at Smyrna. (*Nutuk*, 1985, pp. 9-10)

Succinctly, with a few vivid, terse, well-chosen words, Atatürk sets the stage. In his narrative, unworthy shepherds led a proud empire into a state of abject humiliation. These highly-placed traitors against the people had more in common with their conquerors than they did with their own subjects. The Sultan and his coterie willingly colluded with enemy powers to pillage a subjugated, deeply wounded homeland.

Atatürk had the villains he needed for his drama. Yet, everyone is the hero of his own story. People have reasons for what they do, justifications for their actions. As the visible focus of worldwide Muslim identity, the Sultan had a charge to keep. The office of Sultan/Caliph was not his to lay aside. This emblem of the united *dar es salaam*, the house of Islam, had to be protected, preserved, and maintained. Even the Anatolian heartland mattered less, in the Caliph's eyes, than his own role as a living link that demonstrated and protected the unity of Muslims past and present, local and global.

The Anatolians begged to differ. They did not consider themselves expendable, and most of them followed the Salonika-born hero who spoke and acted on their behalf. However, the numinous stature and status of the Caliph was inextricably blended with the Muslim identity in the minds of many. As one religious leader and enemy of Atatürk's programs wrote:

We want the re-establishment of the Caliphate; we do not want new laws; we are satisfied with the Medshelle (religious law); we shall protect the Medressas, the Tekkes, the pious institutions, the Softahs, the Sheikhs, and their disciples. Be on our side; the party of Mustapha Kemal, having abolished the Caliphate, is breaking Islam into ruins; they will make you into unbelievers, into ghiavers; *they will make you wear hats.* (emphasis added) (Atatürk, 1985, p. 717)

The editor of *Tanin* was also was a passionate advocate for the Caliph:

No great sagacity is necessary to understand that if we lose the Caliphate, the Turkish State, comprising between five and ten million souls, would have no longer any weight in the Mohammedan world, and that we would degrade ourselves in addition in the eyes of European diplomacy to the rank of a small state without any importance.

Is this a national way of thinking? Every Turk who really possesses national feeling must support the Caliphate with all his strength. (Atatürk, 1985, p. 669)

There were reasons for the failures of the Ottoman system. Confronting the root causes of those failures would, Atatürk believed, help his people find a better way. Atatürk was deeply estranged from the central elements of Ottoman culture, and blamed traditional Islam for the woes that had befallen the Turkish people. He responded to his enemies' charge ("They will make you wear hats") with a diatribe against the fez, the traditional Ottoman headgear:

Gentlemen, it was necessary to abolish the fez, which sat on our heads as a sign of ignorance, of fanaticism, of hatred to progress and civilisation [*sic*], and to adopt in its place the hat, the customary head-dress of the whole civilised [*sic*] world, thus showing, among other things, that no difference existed in the manner of thought between the Turkish nation and the whole family of civilised [*sic*] mankind. ...

93

One will be able to imagine how necessary the carrying through of these measures was, in order to prove that our nation as a whole was no primitive nation, filled with superstitions and prejudices. (Atatürk, 1985, p. 720)

In *Nutuk*, Atatürk stressed the need to write off sunk costs. The past is the past. The old order was dead – and justifiably so. The Ottoman Empire was, according to Atatürk, rotten with superstition, backward, paralyzed by tradition, unequal to the demands of modern life, and a source of contemptuous amusement to the imagined audience he played to – those he viewed as the truly civilized, truly modern, truly scientific nations of the West. The ignorance and obdurate stubbornness of the old Ottomans had left the Turkish heartland defenseless, pillaged, in disarray, no longer master of its own destiny. And who was to blame for that? The superstitious people, or the charlatans who catered to their superstitions?

Could a civilised [*sic*] nation tolerate a mass of people who let themselves be led by the nose by a herd of Sheikhs, Dedes, Seids, Tschelebis, Babas and Emirs; who entrusted their destiny and their lives to chiromancers, magicians, dice-throwers and amulet sellers? Ought one to conserve in the Turkish State, in the Turkish Republic, elements and institutions such as those which had for centuries given the nation the appearance of being other than it really was? Would one not therewith have committed the greatest, most irreparable error to the cause of progress and reawakening? If we made use of the law for the Restoration of Order in this manner, it was in order to avoid such a historic error; to show the nation's brow pure and luminous, as it is; to prove that our people think neither in a fanatical nor a reactionary manner. (Atatürk, 1985, p. 610)

94

Atatürk insisted that the Ottoman Empire was bankrupt, broken, demoralized, and obsolete, as a result, in large measure, of the malfeasance of its spiritual leaders. Under his guidance, however, the people made the right choices, jettisoning the trappings and ornamental fetters of cloying tradition, and embracing a new lodestar of existence. Although they still shared a common language, and privately practiced a common religious faith, Turkish public life was defined by a new transcendent principle.

And what were the god-words of this new order, the new transcendent points of reference? For Atatürk, the side of the angels consisted of that which was modern, scientific, and secular. He proclaimed that the nation itself could be its own polestar, if scientifically managed. Kasaba cites Atatürk's paean to progress:

> It is futile to try to resist the thunderous advance of civilization, for it has no pity on those who are ignorant or rebellious. The sublime force of civilization pierces mountains, crosses the skies, enlightens and explores everything from the smallest particle of dust to stars. When faced with this, those nations who try to follow the superstitions of the Middle Ages are condemned to be destroyed or at least to become enslaved and debased. (Kasaba, 2000)

Atatürk, like the Georgian monk who later became Stalin, and the Austrian lad who later became Hitler, had his aspirations shaped by a culture other than the one he was born into. A brief detour through Russia may help us grasp more clearly the underlying motif of Atatürk's passion. In several of his essays, novelist Orhan Pamuk discussed the kindred spirit he encountered in Russian writers. Like the secular Turk, Dostoevsky, Tolstoy, and company experienced an uneasy borderland existence between their own culture and Western

Europe (2008, p. 137). The Russian word *intelligentsia* has entered the English vernacular as a dismissive label for the rootless, pompous, alienated intellectual. In the early 20th century, as the estrangement between people and rulers reached lethal proportions, Soviet citizens desperately yearned to be "somewhere else." Russian American novelist Ayn Rand wrote of the magic word *abroad:*

> The meaning of the word for a Soviet citizen is incommunicable to anyone who has not lived in that country: if you project what you would feel for a combination of Atlantis, the Promised Land and the most glorious civilization on another planet, as imagined by a benevolent kind of science fiction, you will have a pale approximation. "Abroad," to a Soviet Russian, is as distant, shining and unattainable as these; yet to any Russian who lifts his head for a moment from the Soviet muck, the concept "abroad" is a psychological necessity, and lifeline and a soul preserver.
>
> That concept is made of brilliant bits sneaked, smuggled or floating in through the dense gray fog of the foreign movies, magazines, radio broadcasts, or even the clothing and the confident posture of foreign visitors. These bits are so un-Soviet and so alive, that they blend in one's mind into a vision of freedom, abundance, unimaginable technological efficiency and, above all, a sense of joyous, fearless, benevolent gaiety. (Rand, 1970, pp. 121-122)

Yet, the Turkish people had not only shed the old order. They had also whole-heartedly embraced the new order. In a speech cited here, Atatürk waxed lyrical as he described the passions that sustained him, and the nation, through their struggles:

> The duties of the commander-in-chief can at the utmost continue till the day when we shall have attained a decisive

result corresponding to the spirit of the National Pact. There is no doubt that we shall achieve this happy result. On that day our precious town of Smyrna, our beautiful Brusa, our Stambul and our Thrace will all be re-embodied in our mother-country. On that day, together with the nation, we shall live to experience the greatest happiness, and I, for my part, will also realise [*sic*] another joy, namely, that I shall take up the place again which I occupied on the day we began to defend our sacred cause. Is there a nobler joy than to be a free man among a free people? For those who are taking part in the great truths, for those who know no other joys than the moral and sacred delights of the heart and conscience, material dignities, high as they may be have no value. (Atatürk, 2006, p. 485)

The Ottoman Empire assumed that the Caliph was the defender of Islam, and derived his transcendent mandate from that faith. Atatürk, in contrast, asserted the glory of being "a free man among a free people," and "declared that the new source of legitimacy should be 'the people,' whose collective interest should be represented by a new leadership that would usher in a new era and a new consciousness" (Davison, 1998, p. 148). This harkens back to Rousseau's doctrine of the "general will," as incarnated in the rule of the new philosopher kings who could interpret to the people what their will really was. Left to themselves, after all, the people would continue to wallow in ignorance, look foolish to the West, and would be, in Atatürk's words, "a laughingstock in the eyes of the really civilized and cultured people of the world" (Davison, 1998, p. 148).

When Esra Özyürek interviewed "the elderly children of the Republic," people who had come of age during the intoxicating days of the early Turkish republic, she discovered that Atatürk had, indeed, sold his vision to the Turkish people.

These people, in their 80s at the time Özyürek talked with them, recalled their youth as a time of optimism, utopian expectations, and unlimited possibilities. "Atatürk's era was like heaven on earth," said one. A retired university professor reminisced: "Some say Atatürk was a dictator. There was no need for him to be . . . Everyone was so happy in those days. They gave him full support." Four themes frequently appeared in the collected memoirs of this demographic: love and support for Atatürk and his reforms, secularism, peace and unity, and the event that brought the good times to an end: the introduction of multi-party democracy in 1950, and the election of a new party to power (Özyürek, 2006, pp. 49-55).

Atatürk, in his role as a world-changer, convinced a dispirited people that a newer world, a better world, was not only possible, but necessary. So, too, did the Bishop of Hippo, Augustine.

Augustine and the first theme.

Augustine dealt with the Roman Empire, a social order that was founded on fratricide, rotten with pagan superstition, and clearly unequal to the demands of the day. The barbarian hoards had started by nibbling around the edges, but eventually strode triumphantly into the urban heart of the empire. Even though this invasion broke the hearts of those whose identity was so heavily invested in that order, Augustine asserted, Romulus's city was an ugly order, and deserved to die. The Roman Empire had hitched its wagon to the wrong star, a falling star.

Atatürk was a secular leader of a religious nation, who viewed the faith of his people as a problem to overcome. Augustine was a Christian pastor with a more straightforward task. Augustine's God was unambiguously and forthrightly the Christian deity, the God defined in the orthodox creeds of the church, the God who had intervened in such a powerful way in his own life, and who was worshipped by Christians of all social strata in places throughout the Roman Empire.

Yet, since Augustine wished to persuade responsible pagans, he dealt in depth with the faith of these people. He spent the first five books of the *City of God* refuting the notion that the adoration of the pagan gods had value in terms of earthly benefits conferred upon the worshippers. The gods of Rome, he pointed out, were often transplants from realms that Rome had overrun. Many of the Roman gods were used goods, such as the hand-me-down deities of Troy, Ileum, and Alba, three cities Rome erased. These gods, which had been unable to protect their own people, were then revered by the victors who had razed their previous worshipers.

Augustine then discusses the ethical component of paganism. Could the pagan deities lead those who served them to lead more righteous lives on Earth, and to hope for a blessed afterlife? Augustine, who had evidently been an avid theatergoer in his youth, took savage delight in ridiculing the plays that the Romans used in the service of their older religion. These theatrical spectacles depicted the gods doing things that any self-respecting human would blush to undertake:

> Does not the society of wicked men pollute our life if they insinuate themselves into our affections and win our assent and does not the society of demons pollute our life, who are worshipped with their own crimes? If with true crimes, how wicked the demons! If with false, how wicked the worship! (City, VI, 6)

> If these are sacred rites, what is sacrilege? If this is purification, what is pollution? (City, II, 4)

Even in terms of routine, everyday competence, Augustine wrote, the Roman gods fell short. You can trust one man, a porter, to keep a door, since he is a man. It takes three pagan gods to perform the same task – "Forculus to the doors, Cardea to the hinge, Limentinus to the threshold" (City, IV, 8).

In one of the most exquisitely sarcastic passages found in ancient literature, Augustine discusses the gods of the wedding chamber, enumerating their names and functions, arriving at last at the goddess Pertunda. He then asks the obvious question, "What has the goddess Pertunda to do there? Let her blush; let her go forth. Let the husband himself do something. It is disgraceful that any one but himself should do that from which she gets her name" (City, VI, 9).

Obviously, the source of Roman morality had to be sought in something other than its putative religion. The Roman gods were, Augustine wrote, unworthy of the honor rendered them. The Romans, in their days of greatness, held themselves to higher standards of conduct than they expected of their gods. If they could not look to the heavens for the wellsprings of their greatness, what did inspire their noble achievements? Augustine concluded that the world-bestriding imperial Romans were driven by a love of "glory."

> Glory they most ardently loved; for it they wished to live, for it they did not hesitate to die. Every other desire was repressed by the strength of their passion for that one thing. At length, because it seemed inglorious to serve, but glorious to rule and to command, they first earnestly desired to be free, and then to be mistress. (City, V, 12)

> At that time it was their greatest ambition either to die bravely or to live free; but when liberty was obtained, so great a desire of glory took possession of them, that liberty

alone was not enough unless domination also would be sought. These arts they exercised with the more skill the less they gave themselves up to pleasures, and to enervation of body and mind in amassing riches. (City, V, 12)

Not all vices are created equal. Some debilitate, while others spur the vicious person or society to achieve notable exploits, heroic endeavors.

However, in terms of power to ennoble life in the present, and to afford devotees hope for the future life, the God adored by orthodox Christians had achieved a credibility that even nostalgic pagans could only rue. The old gods might be cherished family heirlooms, but the present and future belonged to the Lord Christ. "And whoever now-a-days demands to see prodigies that he may believe, is himself a great prodigy, because he does not believe, though the whole world does," Augustine wrote in Book XXII, Chapter 8.

Atatürk and Augustine both offered their audiences a transcendent frame of reference, a basis for believing that things could, and should, be other than as they were at the moment.

The Second Principle: Clearly Identify the Rival Teams

In the low-budget Australian movie *The Return of Captain Invincible*, the embittered and disillusioned title character played by Alan Arkin sings this cynical dirge:

Now who's wearing black hats and who's wearing white,

And who's on the side of justice and right.

The line is so fine between Heaven and Hell,

Not even a hero can tell.

The good guys from the bad guys. (Mora, 1983)

Skeptics can easily point out the foibles of the agents of the old order, even as they are unable to suggest any alternative. Jonathan Swift's scatological *Gulliver's Travels* and Voltaire's *Candide* both lampoon the pillars of the current regime, but in such a way as to leave the reader disgruntled, and sometimes disgusted, rather than inspired. A defter satirist can lampoon William Jennings Bryan, "the lion of the prairies," the gold standard, and greenbacks, with such a sly and amusing parable that people still chuckle at "the little man behind the curtain" generations after they forget the monetary policy issues that inspired *The Wizard of Oz* (Baum, 1979).

The old regime, the failed social order, has its vested interests, forces that would rather see their nation in ruins than cede an inch of personal prestige, status, and position. Yet, these vested interests derive much of their influence from their solidarity. Obviously, those who would supplant them also need to work with like-minded allies. And yes, a real hero can tell "the good guys from the bad guys."

Team Atatürk (and rivals).

After the dramatic introduction to Nutuk, Atatürk kept the momentum of his narrative going with a detailed account of the steps he took to assemble his team. When Hıfzı Velidedeoğlu translated Nutuk into modern Turkish, he added chapter titles. Chapter 3 introduces the National Congresses (Ulusal Kongreler) Atatürk convened in Ankara, in the heart of the Anatolian heartland, far from the corrupting dead hand of the failed order cowering in İstanbul. The title of Chapter 4 makes clear exactly who wore the black hats:

> *Damat Ferit Paşa hükümeti dünaminde yerli hayınlarla uğraşmalar.*
> (Damat Ferit Pasha's government during the time of the local insurrections and struggles)

As the counterpart to the various "official" governments organized by the lackeys of the sultan and the foreign powers the Sublime Porte colluded with, Atatürk summoned patriotic delegates to a national gathering in the hitherto obscure town of Angora, present-day Ankara. The initials T. B. M. M. do not appear in several standard Turkish/English dictionaries, and need no definition in Turkish history books. *Türkiye Büyük Millet Meclisi* (the Turkish Grand National Assembly) entered history and legend as the birthplace of the modern Turkish republic, even as the American Constitutional Convention defined an earlier new nation. Team Atatürk was coming together.

Atatürk minced no words when heaping contempt and scorn upon the heads of "the degenerate occupant of the throne," and his handlers and enablers. The Sultan, he asserted, had forfeited his right to speak for the nation when he consented to the desecration of his nation. Atatürk, a soldier and a leader of soldiers, was unsparing in his praise of the heroism of Mehmetçik, the stalwart Turkish infantryman. The losses of the last century, he asserted, could not be laid at the feet of those who'd fought to preserve the empire. Rather, the blame must be assigned to those who mismanaged the empire, betrayed the people who were counting upon them for wise and relevant leadership, and foolishly meddled in the tribal quarrels of alien powers.

Like Oliver Cromwell, an earlier military leader who translated success in battle into a new form of government, Atatürk relied heavily upon fellow members of the old empire's military elite (Paul, 1964). Good leaders in battle were entrusted with power in civil government. For example, Colonel İsmet's success at the First Battle of İnönü established the credibility of the Turkish resistance, and paved the way for the Treaty of Moscow (Atatürk, 1985, p. 459). When Atatürk compelled the Turks to adopt surnames, this politically-active military hero named himself for the battle, and as İsmet İnönü took the reins of power upon Atatürk's death (Kinross, 1965, p. 4).

Atatürk may have midwifed the modern Turkish republic, but he did not work alone. Neither did Augustine.

Team Augustine (and rivals).

In the turmoil surrounding the fall of Rome, Augustine wrote his magnum opus as a means of encouragement to his fellow Romans. Yes, their empire had fallen on hard times. However, the wise man did not put all his eggs in one rotten basket. The wise man did not pin his hopes upon a fallible, and corrupt, human commonwealth. The wise man participated joyfully in an alternate reality, an alternate polity, an alternate community.

So, what is a "city"? Augustine proposes a useful definition:

> But if we . . . say that a people is an assemblage of reasonable beings bound together by a common agreement as to the objects of their love, then, in order to discover the character of any people, we have only to observe what they love. Yet whatever it loves, if only it is an assemblage of reasonable beings and not of beasts, and is bound together by an agreement as to the objects of love, it is reasonably called a people; and it will be a superior people in proportion as it is bound together by higher interests, inferior in proportion as it is bound together by lower. (City, XIX, 24)

The city of God, Augustine wrote, predated the creation of the earth, and had as its first citizens the holy angels of God (City, XI, 9). It is defined by allegiance to God, even as the city of man is defined by the love of self.

> Accordingly, two cities have been formed by two loves: the earthly by the love of self, even to the

contempt of God; the heavenly by the love of God, even to the contempt of self. The former, in a word, glories in itself, the latter in the Lord. For the one seeks glory from men; but the greatest glory of the other is God, the witness of conscience. The one lifts up its head in its own glory; the other says to its God, "Thou art my glory, and the lifter up of mine head." In the one, the princes and the nations it subdues are ruled by the love of ruling; in the other, the princes and the subjects serve one another in love, the latter obeying, while the former take thought for all. The one delights in its own strength, represented in the persons of its rulers; the other says to its God, "I will love Thee, O Lord, my strength." (City, XIV, 28)

The two cities do not, however, inhabit different geographical spheres, or wear distinctive uniforms. Citizens of both cities rub elbows in the course of everyday life. However, they are distinguished from each other by the quality of their lives and loves.

Team Augustine, like Team Atatürk, also had its influential citizens and shapers, its saints, bishops, and martyrs. Atatürk and Augustine were simultaneously coaches and team players, who achieved much through both building upon, and inspiring the work of the others.

The Third Principle: Ethics

Expediency has no power to summon the loyalty of people to charge the barricades. Those who would carve their initials on history must be able to conjure up that kind of passion. Communism was an odious ideology that somehow appealed to the noblest instincts of the best people, even as it placed the "more equal" people in command (Orwell, 1993, p. 88).

Douglas Hyde reports the motivational speech given to Viet Cong soldiers sent to overrun Dien Bien Phu:

> You will almost certainly die. Already, even to get within gun range, you have to clamber and slither over men's rotting bodies, the bodies of your own comrades. The probability is that you will die, just as they have done. If you do, you will not just be dying in the fight against French colonialism. You will not just be dying for Vietnam. You will be dying for suffering, oppressed humanity all over the world. Your death will help to make the world a better place. (Hyde, 1966, p. 149)

Even people without a deity to invoke yearn for significance, and aspire to be a part of something bigger than themselves. As the various anti-colonial movements and brushfire wars of the 20th century demonstrated, nationalism can motivate both stunning atrocities and real heroism.

Which ethical imperatives informed the messages of Atatürk and Augustine?

The ethics of Atatürk.

In several of his more famous military orders, Atatürk summoned his troops to make the ultimate effort. At Gallipolis he wrote: "I don't order you to attack, I order you to die. In the time it takes us to die, other troops and commanders can come and take our places." Kinross tells the rest of the story: "By the end of the battle almost the whole of the 57th Regiment had died, charging continuously through a curtain of enemy rifle fire to win immortality in the annals of the Turkish army" (1965, p. 90).

Somewhere, somehow, the successful change agent must be able to point towards a standard of behavior that provides a rationale for sacrificial actions, and permits true nobility.

People hunger for significance, after all. In Atatürk's cosmology, the unified Turkish national republic was the *summum bonum*, the ultimate good, and the collective reality that would make possible the noblest of personal living. The nation was a good so worthy it was worth dying for.

A clear-cut standard of ethics has both its positive and negative poles. If that which contributes to the union and health of the nation is the ultimate good, then factions must be the ultimate evil. This conviction resonated with Atatürk's audience, since it reflected a deeply rooted traditional *bête noire*. To this day, Muslim clerics treat divisiveness (*fitna*) as the ultimate evil. Peace will only come when all of humanity is united under the one green banner of Islam. Such was the thrust of an apparently typical sermon preached at a Durham, NC mosque.

Fitna: A vignette.

The guest shifted uncomfortably on the carpeted concrete floor for the better part of an hour. He noted the horizontal stripes, spaced approximately five feet apart, angled at an inexplicable vector to the walls. The imam, a bearded young Egyptian who spoke flawless English, exhorted his flock with a message that would be mostly acceptable in any Christian pulpit: on the need to guard one's family and faith from the corrosive effects of the surrounding culture. From time to time, the speaker chanted a few verses in Arabic, with a resonant, perfectly pitched voice. One Arabic word kept recurring in his sermon: *fitna*. This was obviously something very bad, something to be avoided at all costs, something that would discredit the message of Islam even as it destroyed the Islamic community. He finished his sermon, and the crowd stood, elbow-to-elbow on the stripes in the carpet, facing Mecca, and went through the postures of Muslim prayer. The guest reflected upon this vice that appeared so heinous to the speaker that it was worth dedicating an hour-long message to.

Further research revealed that *fitna* meant divisiveness. In particular, *fitna* referred to the bloody interregnum that befell Islam a few generations after Mohammed's death, and resulted in the splits between Shiite and Sunni that persist to this day. Apparently, the unity of the community is something so imperative in the Islamic ethos that divisiveness needs to be suppressed at all costs.

The genius of Atatürk lay in refocusing this moral imperative away from an abstract, global community and on to the concrete Turkish nation, defined by Turkish geography, language, and culture. The ethical imperative Atatürk preached was the integrity and health of the nation: That which is good for the nation is good, and that which threatens the integrity, the wholeness, of the nation is bad.

This passion shows up throughout *Nutuk*. In the beginning of the speech, Atatürk dwells at length on the perfidy of the Sultan and his coterie, who were willing participants in the planned dismemberment of the Turkish heartland. As the history of the Turkish social revolution continues, Atatürk deals decisively with other divisive forces – the conservative Muslim establishment, restive Kurds, and bitter Christian minorities. He lived the ideal, and reached the climax of his public life with a unified nation to bequeath to "the youth of Turkey."

Although his personal moral failures are widely acknowledged – the founder of modern Turkey died of cirrhosis of the liver – Atatürk's message had a sincerely-believed ethical component that resonated with his audience. Augustine was canonized; his message, too, relied heavily upon its intrinsic ethical merits.

The ethics of Augustine.

Augustine pointed to that distillation of Christian life and practice, the city of God, that community of those whose lives bear the imprint of a superior moral order. The city of God is, first and foremost, from, by, and about God. Citizens of this heavenly community are loved by God, love God more than self, and love others for the sake of the God who loved and redeemed them. Although lesser loves might bring a measure of earthly happiness, or earthly achievement, nothing less than God Himself will satisfy in the long run. In a colorful metaphor, Augustine talks about the source of true felicity:

> But if Felicity is not a goddess, because, as is true, it is a gift of God, that god must be sought who has power to give it, and that hurtful multitude of false gods must be abandoned which the vain multitude of foolish men follows after, making gods to itself of the gifts of God, and offending Himself whose gifts they are by the stubbornness of a proud will. For he cannot be free from infelicity who worships Felicity as a goddess, and forsakes God, the giver of felicity; just as he cannot be free from hunger who licks a painted loaf of bread, and does not buy it of the man who has a real one. (City, IV, 23)

The ethics of Augustine begin with that which is due to God – worship, adoration, and obedience. His ethics go on to include that which is due to people – justice, tempered by humility. Yet, even in the context of human relationships, only the reality of God, and His standards, make justice possible. "But the fact is, true justice has no existence save in that republic whose founder and ruler is Christ" (City, II, 21).

Like Atatürk, Augustine had little patience with those who sought excuses for schism. The Donatists of Africa saw much of their credibility evaporate beneath the blowtorch heat of Augustine's barbed wit and busy pen.

The Fourth Principle: Public Commitments

Atatürk's diplomacy.

Every corporate entity is defined by the commitments it makes, the commitments it breaks, and the commitments it binds its members to. For this reason, Nutuk gives a great deal of thought and space to discussing the treaties that developed and grew up around the waning days of the Ottoman Empire and the early days of the Turkish Republic.

Atatürk did not begin his work of nation building in a vacuum. He inherited the fallout from four secret agreements that various European powers had made about the future of Turkey without consulting the Turks: the Constantinople agreement (1915), the Secret Treaty of London (1915), the Sykes-Picot Agreement (1916), and the St. Jean de Maurienne Agreement (1916) (Lewis, 1960, pp. 48-49; Kinross, 1965, p. 164). These furtive plots to divide the Turkish heartland into various spheres of political and economic influence lend credence to Augustine's cynical observation that unjust governments are large-scale criminal syndicates (Augustine, IV, 4).

Matters did not improve for the nation, Atatürk argued, when the obsequious lackeys surrounding the Sublime Porte decided that their privileges trumped the good of the Turkish people. The European victors had found quislings who were willing to give the color of legality to their depredations, native token "leaders" who would affix their signatures to the documents they were handed. Atatürk discussed this perfidy in one of his famous "open letter" telegrams sent to various military commands and loyal local governing bodies:

> On account of the reactionary attitude of the Government and in order to secure the defence [sic] of our rights in these most dangerous days through which we are passing, the

election and speedy meeting of a National Assembly is our most urgent duty to undertake.

The Government has deceived the people and has postponed the elections from month to month. In the same manner, on different pretexts, it has postponed the execution of the order it had eventually issued. The Note which Ferid Pasha has just laid before the Peace Conference shows that he will surrender our vilayets beyond the Taurus.

His next step, which will be to make the frontier line pass through the Vilayet of Smyrna – after having previously come to an agreement with the Greeks – distinctly shows his intention of giving up the territory already occupied by the Greeks.

Last of all, the thoughtless and malicious policy pursued by him in other occupied parts of the country, enables us to foresee in a similar way that he will expose the country and the nation to dismemberment and confront them with an accomplished fact by signing the Peace Treaty before the National Assembly can meet. (Atatürk, 2006, p. 90)

While the Sultan and his court continued treating with the victors of The Great War, Atatürk, the military, the Grand National Assembly, and the local "Unions for the Defence of the Rights" withheld their consent. Shortly after the Greek armies, despite their superior equipment, were halted at the First Battle of İnönü, Russia broke ranks with the other European powers and negotiated a separate peace. The new Bolshevik regime had worries of its own, and signed the Treaty of Moscow on March 13, 1921 (Atatürk, 2006, p. 362).

When the European powers began dealing with the Grand National Assembly, they initially tried to treat with both Turkish governments – the monarchy and the Republic – as equally legitimate peers. Atatürk complained vehemently.

After the Sultan was dethroned, the point became moot, and the Treaty of Lausanne recognized the new realities on the ground.

Augustine's diplomacy.

Augustine may not have conducted formal negotiations at conference tables, but his explanation of the relationships between the two cities, between the realm of Caesar and the realm of Jesus, between state and church, continues to shape public discourse 1,500 years later.

Although he heaped withering scorn upon the deities of Rome, Augustine regarded the pagans as people who deserved to be treated with respect. As a gifted scholar, Augustine could describe in detail the rationales behind the various forms of Roman piety: civil, religious, poetic. In a long paragraph that pulls together the main strands of Augustine's polemic against Rome's gods and civil religion, he directly but kindly challenges Varro to rethink his positions on these matters:

> O Marcus Varro! thou art the most acute, and without doubt the most learned, but still a man, not God – now lifted up by the Spirit of God to see and to announce divine things, thou seest, indeed, that divine things are to be separated from human trifles and lies, but thou fearest to offend those most corrupt opinions of the populace, and their customs in public superstitions, which thou thyself, when thou considerest them on all sides, perceivest, and all your literature loudly pronounces to be abhorrent from the nature of the gods, even of such gods as the frailty of the human mind supposes to exist in the elements of this world. What can the most excellent human talent do here? What can human learning, though manifold, avail thee in this perplexity? Thou desirest to worship the natural gods; thou art compelled to worship the civil. Thou hast found some of

the gods to be fabulous, on whom thou vomitest forth very freely what thou thinkest, and, whether thou willest or not, thou wettest therewith even the civil gods. Thou sayest, forsooth, that the fabulous are adapted to the theatre, the natural to the world, and the civil to the city; though the world is a divine work, but cities and theatres are the works of men, and though the gods who are laughed at in the theatre are not other than those who are adored in the temples; and ye do not exhibit games in honor of other gods than those to whom ye immolate victims. How much more freely and more subtly wouldst thou have decided these hadst thou said that some gods are natural, others established by men; and concerning those who have been so established, the literature of the poets gives one account, and that of the priests another – both of which are, nevertheless, so friendly the one to the other, through fellowship in falsehood, that they are both pleasing to the demons, to whom the doctrine of the truth is hostile. (City, VI, 6)

A modern writer could summarize and paraphrase this section: "My excellent friend, you are embarrassed by your own gods, even when you try to cherry-pick the useful ones from the filthy ones." Juggling civic, poetic, and natural deities, defending some, while reviling others, is a lost cause. These mental gymnastics take more effort than any reasonable man would invest in such a problematic enterprise. Yes, the traditional gods may have been the binding mental and emotional framework of the old order. But, since the old order is gone anyhow, why not take the opportunity to jettison those dead weights?

In books XVII through XIX, Augustine displayed his mastery of secular history, discussing the developments of civil and religious institutions in Egypt, Babylon, Greece, and Rome. As he discussed this timeline, he interleaved the chronologies of the Old Testament kings and prophets. The city of God, he thus demonstrated, was not an ethereal state of timeless *gnosis*, but a solid historical reality, involving real people doing real deeds at real points in time.

Early in this work, in Book V, Augustine discussed the interactions and intersections of the two cities in the persons of various Christian Roman emperors and their foes. The most blessed emperors, he asserted, were those who used their power to advance God's kingdom, who abstained from rapacious behavior and overbearing dictates, who first ruled over themselves. (City, V, 24)

Augustine and Atatürk were both men of their times, who had messages that powerfully influenced the contemporary audiences they wrote for. However, both men envisioned their beloved community as surviving their day, and extending into the indefinite, but glorious, future.

The Fifth Principle: The Basis for Continuity

Atatürk and continuity.

In a stirring conclusion to a national epic, Atatürk speaks directly to his immediate audience:

> Gentlemen, I have taken trouble to show, in these accounts, how a great people, whose national course was considered as ended, reconquered its independence; how it created a national and modern State founded on the latest results of science.

> The result we have attained today is the fruit of teachings which arose from centuries of suffering, and the price of streams of blood which have drenched every foot of the ground of our beloved Fatherland.

114

This holy treasure I lay in the hands of the youth of Turkey.
(Atatürk, 2006, p. 610)

He then utters his memorable challenge to the living and future youth of Turkey, in a passionate oration that Turkish schoolchildren still memorize and recite, even as American schoolchildren once memorized the Gettysburg Address:

Turkish Youth! your primary duty is ever to preserve and defend the National independence, the Turkish Republic.

That is the only basis of your existence and your future. This basis contains your most precious treasure. In the future, too, there will be ill-will, both in the country itself and abroad, which will try to tear this treasure from you. If one day you are compelled to defend your independence and the Republic, then, in order to fulfill your duty, you will have to look beyond the possibilities and conditions in which you might find yourself. It may be that these conditions and possibilities are altogether unfavourable. It is possible that the enemies who desire to destroy your independence and your Republic represent the strongest force that the earth has ever seen; that they have, through craft and force, taken possession of all the fortresses and arsenals of the fatherland; that all its armies are scattered and the country actually and completely occupied.

Assuming, in order to look still darker possibilities in the face, that those who hold the power of Government within the country have fallen into error, that they are fools or traitors, yes, even that these leading, persons, identify their personal interests with the enemy's political goals, in might happen that the nation came into complete privation, into the most extreme distress; that it found itself in a condition, of ruin and complete exhaustion.

Even under those circumstances, O Turkish child of future generations! It is your duty to save the independence, the Turkish Republic.

The strength that you will need for this is mighty in the noble blood which flows in your veins. (Atatürk, 2006, p. 611-612)

In Atatürk's perspective, military service was synonymous with continuity. The willingness of the youth of Turkey to serve in the armed forces of their nation, to "make of their breasts a shield for the nation," was the guarantor of this republic's future. He apparently viewed the military as embodying all that was most noble, and most professional, in Turkish culture. The military reciprocated this confidence, and viewed it as their mission to protect the modern, secular, Turkish republic from all enemies, foreign or domestic.

Augustine and continuity.

Marcus Varro, the scholar and writer Augustine addressed, and the prudent magistrates he also had in mind, have long since joined him in the dust. Yet Augustine assumed that the city of God would continue. He imagined a mechanism for ensuring the continuity of this entity. Somehow, the God of this city would continue incorporating people into this ongoing project, so they could each play their brief roles in turn. For Augustine, the sacrament of baptism incorporated people into the city of God and the grace of God. In a number of passages, he spoke of "the font of regeneration," and of miracles that had happened when people went through the waters of baptism (City, XXII, 8).

The word *sacrament* is derived from the Latin word *sacramentum*. *Cassell's New Latin Dictionary* (Simpson, 1960) defines *sacramentum* as "the engagement entered into by newly enlisted soldiers, the military oath of allegiance." Those who submit to

Christian baptism enlist in a life-long struggle against the world, the flesh, and the devil, but they do not fight alone. They serve under the banner of a glorious Commander, follow the inspiring examples of heroes of the past, shoulder to shoulder with God's people today, and anticipate final victory as the outcome of their lives.

Atatürk and Augustine both rejoiced in their bright hopes for a world they would not live to see. Both were confident that their efforts would propagate forward through time to redirect the course of history, and continue to protect those in the community they had given their lives to.

Chapter Summary

For this chapter, we have selected one useful tool from a parallel academic discipline that appeared useful for the purposes of this paper. Having previously argued that *City of God* and *Nutuk* are members of a specific genre – blueprints for redefining social reality – we borrowed from the discipline of theology a paradigm that works well for other such documents. We then discussed the ways in which Atatürk and Augustine dealt with five major themes: transcendent purpose, hierarchies, ethics, covenants, and succession. Both of these world makers provided substantive answers to those questions, answers that their audiences found convincing.

Transcendent purpose.

When we are overwhelmed by events, we can find it nearly impossible to look beyond the screaming demands of the moment. Survival trumps aesthetics, and nearly everything else. However, successful world-changers can direct our attention to a larger frame of reference.

Atatürk held before his audience the vision of national prestige, a modern nation that could treat as an equal with all the other modern powers. This ideal combined a pride in Turkish culture with an admiration for the achievements of the West.

Augustine assured his readers that God was bigger than Caesar, and the city of God both predated and would long outlive the city of man. By faith, people could bet their lives on a more durable kingdom, one that could not be shaken, even as the kingdoms of this world crumbled around their ears.

Hierarchies.

People need to know their position in the social order, where they stand, who stands with them, and who stands against them. Successful world-changers are team players who take leading roles, but do not act alone.

Atatürk made it clear to his audience who the enemy was – the discredited imperial court, the Sublime Porte, which had betrayed the interests of the Turkish people in order to make common cause with the enemies of the nation. True and faithful leadership, however, could be found in the ranks of the professional military establishment, the valiant warriors who defended the nation with their own lives.

Augustine reminded his Christian readers that the hierarchy of the Catholic Church endured. In fact, even the barbarian invaders respected the properties of the church, and honored the right of sanctuary for those who took shelter in Christian buildings (City, I, ch. 1). The prestige of the Christian organization had been secured by the routine charity and holiness of individual lay members, and underlined by the heroic martyrdoms of the saints.

Ethics.

What lodestone can people use as a quick way to weight decisions in a stressful time? What pocket magnet can instantly distinguish between sound metal auto body and Bondo-concealed damage?

For Atatürk, the integrity of the Turkish people, reposing in a secure heartland, was the governing criteria. Those who fought for this united homeland were on the side of the angels. Those who traded in portions of their patria and patrimony for personal opulence were, obviously, on the other side.

For Augustine, a willingness to love God and neighbor more than self defined heaven and characterized the citizens of heaven who happened to be residing currently, and temporarily, on earth.

Covenants.

Atatürk paid a great deal of attention to the various treaties, the formal commitments, which framed the discourse of Nutuk. Secret treaties provoked the War of Salvation (*Kurtulu Savaşı*) by imposing unacceptable conditions upon the Turks, and by dismembering the nation. The Turks stood tall among the nations when they pushed back and forcefully asserted their own terms, their own interests, through formally recognized treaties.

Augustine described the formal covenants God made throughout history with his people, and the fate of secular rulers who either honored, or persecuted, the citizens of God's city.

Succession.

Nutuk is a book of wars that presents military service as the guarantor of national survival. In his stirring address to the youth of Turkey, Atatürk calls upon them, if necessary, to "make of their breasts a shield for the nation."

Augustine celebrated the sacraments, especially baptism, as formal enlistments in the ongoing life of the city of God. A sacrament, like a soldier's oath of enlistment, commits him to the struggle in progress, for the duration of hostilities.

Bottom Line.

Two writers and opinion leaders, a 5th-century African Christian and a 20th-century secular Muslim, summoned desperate people to heroic efforts that successfully remade their broken worlds. They answered the big questions persuasively, redeemed their situations, and left an enduring legacy of beneficent paradigm-setting.

Chapter 4: A Quantitative Exploration

Overview

In the first three chapters, we argued that *Nutuk* is an important work by a significant historical figure. Both the document and its author deserve wider recognition. Kemal Atatürk redefined his world, and reshaped his culture. This places him in a select group, an elite company. As a leader, teacher, and articulate writer, Atatürk persuaded a nation to embrace a radically altered vision of who they were as a people. He defined a social order that outlived him, one that continues to garner positive recognition from observers around the world.

Turks and communication scholars from other nations recognize *Nutuk* as the central repository of this new societal vision. There is convincing agreement on the significance of this document. But what made it so effective? Again, the purpose of this study is to compare *Nutuk* to another masterpiece, Augustine's *City of God*, which also redeemed a chaotic situation. This study is interested in the common elements these documents share. A 5th-century African Christian and a 20th-century modern Turk both redefined the social universes their peers inhabited. What can we learn from what they did?

In Chapter 3, we used a qualitative approach, applying a plausible paradigm to examine both documents. In terms of similar themes employed by influential leaders facing similar crises, *Nutuk* and *City* can be considered members of a very specific genre. Empires can endure for centuries, and typically leave chaos and catastrophe in their wake when they collapse. A strong leader, a Marshall Tito, can forge a micro-empire from an assemblage of "south Slavs" who share little beyond geography, but upon his exit from the scene, the world acquires a new phrase: *ethnic cleansing*. The Afrikaner state can "protect" the separate identities and separate privilege levels of dozens of tribes, black and white, which share a common piece of beloved country, but the end of *apartheid* gives way to global leadership in per-capita rates of murder and rape.

Bringing down an empire is a simple matter, compared to the challenge of building something viable to replace it. Augustine and Atatürk were equal to that challenge. Few others ever were.

For this chapter, we use computerized data processing to support the insights discussed earlier. If the initial assumption of this study is correct, and the five-point treaty model does indeed reveal valid points of comparison between *Nutuk* (hereafter referred to as Nutuk in this chapter) and *City of God* (hereafter referred to as City in this chapter), then a properly calibrated software tool should be able to lend objective and quantitative support to this thesis.

In the previous chapter, we compared Nutuk and City to one another, using a convenient paradigm. The point has now been argued that these are two comparable documents. Therefore, we will use a different approach in this chapter. Since City has been studied for more than 1,500 years, we will consider that task complete. There is little in the way of fresh or original insights we can realistically hope to add to the study of that document. We will therefore use City as a *tool* of analysis, rather than as a *subject* of analysis. Augustine's masterpiece can be a means to an end, a measuring rod to help us better understand Nutuk. Since City has so profoundly influenced western civilization, we might call that book a "gold standard," a paradigm that would-be blueprints for new social orders need to be measured against.

To refine the value of the software-generated data, we will apply the same tools to a classical text that also aspired to reinvent society, but failed at the task. Even as the Catholic and the Protestant find it easier to appreciate their areas of shared perspective when they bring a Mormon into the conversation, the points of agreement between Augustine and Atatürk can be clarified even more when Plato is consulted. The Procrustean blueprint found in Plato's *Republic* (hereafter referred to as Republic in this chapter) provides a number of points of contrast with both Nutuk and City. We can use the repugnant Republic as a companion tool, a "fool's gold standard," for several reasons: antiquity, credibility, and uselessness. In significant ways, Republic belongs to a different genre, and can be expected to use the key terms differently. This parallax will provide the perspective needed to usefully organize the otherwise tautological comparison of the first two documents.

Republic starts with a body of theory, and then considers techniques to fit humanity to the plan. Nutuk and City each start with a given historical crisis, and then provide guidelines for those who wish to master events rather than to be mastered by them. Both of these commended works appeal to those who would surf the waves of change to a newer, better situation.

Republic divides people into rulers and ruled. In words eerily prescient of the Cambodian forced emptying of cities, Socrates offered this recipe for creating the ideal society:

> They will begin by sending out into the country all the inhabitants of the city who are more than ten years old, and will take possession of their children, who will be unaffected by the habits of their parents; these they will train in their own habits and laws, I mean in the laws which we have given them: and in this way the State and constitution of which we

123

were speaking will soonest and most easily attain happiness, and the nation which has such a constitution will gain most. (Republic, VII)

In Plato's report of the conversation, the disputants "arrived at the conclusion that in the perfect State wives and children are to be in common," a notion that has appealed to many later crafters of utopias, (Republic, VIII; Harcourt-Rivington, 2009).

Nutuk and City seek to empower people to master their own situations and better rule their own lives. Republic suggests that rulers are justified in using a deliberate falsehood, a "golden lie."

> Citizens, we shall say to them in our tale, you are brothers, yet God has framed you differently. Some of you have the power of command, and in the composition of these he has mingled gold, wherefore also they have the greatest honour; others he has made of silver, to be auxillaries; others again who are to be husbandmen and craftsmen he has composed of brass and iron; and the species will generally be preserved in the children. (Republic, p. III)

Nutuk and City both assume that the truth is glorious enough to enlist the eager and full cooperation of those who hear it.

Republic envisions a static end-point. Nutuk and City both deal with a process that is in flux, with total chaos as a real possibility. However, real progress, real transformation, are also live options. The future is hopeful, not fixed.

Specialized text-analysis software and generic database and spreadsheet software permit us to compare Nutuk to City, and highlight some of the emphases these two documents share. Given these contrasts between the pragmatic works we are focusing on, and Plato's theory-laden speculations, the numbers should be different, indeed.

In this chapter, we will look at the basic concepts underlying content analysis. We will then explain the rationale for choosing the software tools used. In the interests of full disclosure, we will discuss a preliminary attempt to apply these tools to the task. Unless used with precision, computerized content analysis can simply produce a list of interesting words, and opportunities for self-indulgent *eisogesis*. Increased rigor, and more sophisticated data processing techniques, made the process used for this iteration of the project, the results obtained, and the conclusions drawn from those results more defensible in a scholarly forum.

History and Issues of Content Analysis

Content analysts stick labels on different parts of a textual artifact, and then measure and compare the quantity of words, column inches, airtime, or other discrete quanta occupied by each of the labeled themes. Since ecclesiastical traditions revere words, this technique was pioneered in religious environments. The first scholars to analyze newspapers for their impact on the lives of the readers were pursuing Doctorates of Divinity in the 17th century (Krippendorf, 2004, p. 3). A century later, Swedish churchmen applied content analysis to a controversial new hymnal, and demonstrated that it did not digress to a significant extent from the thematic weighting of the prior official Lutheran hymnal (Krippendorf, 2004, p. 4).

Toward the end of the 19th century, content analysis focused on the perils of the yellow press, and sounded the alarm over the rising tide of sensationalism. During World War II, content analysis of German radio broadcasts teased out the issues most on the minds of the German leadership. By summarizing the sacrifices the people were being exhorted to brace for, Allied scholars were able to detect shifts in military campaigns (Krippendorf, 2004, p. 9).

Content analysis became a useful tool for a number of different scholarly disciplines, including anthropology, psychology, and sociology. Content analysis can deal with large masses of material, and probe issues, and people, in an unobtrusive fashion. This is the only viable approach when the sources of the content are not available for personal interaction. For example, the writer or speaker might be dead, working for the enemy, or protected by doctor/patient confidentiality. When carefully and rigorously conducted, content analysis is unobtrusive and context-sensitive (Krippendorf, pp. 40-42).

Quantitative and qualitative approaches.

A pioneer in this form of research, Klaus Krippendorf, defines content analysis as follows:

> Content analysis is a research technique for making replicable and valid inferences from texts (or other meaningful matter) to the contexts of their use. At its best, content analysis allows the researcher to perform replicable research. He is more than just a critic, evaluating a body of content. (Krippendorf, p. 18)

Whether we approach the body of information from the direction of semiotics, hermeneutics, or traditional communication research, Krippendorf writes, we can operationalize the process "of moving from texts to the contexts of the texts' use." Even though ethnographers may object, it is the researcher who defines the context (Krippendorf, p. 25). Krippendorf writes that the researcher creates "analytical constructs" to formally define, to operationalize the contexts that provide the basis for the inferences derived from the material (pp. 34-35).

Qualitative approaches to content analysis allow more scope for subjectivity. The researchers become part of the measurement apparatus, flagging items that catch their attention. There is value in this approach, as the human mind has powerful and intuitive faculties for detecting patterns. However, as the "face on Mars" demonstrates, the mind can also see patterns that are not there.

Since content analysis is largely a process of counting, measuring, and tabulating, every form of this research technique does have a pronounced quantitative aspect.

Conceptual foundations for text analysis.

The basic assumption of content analysis asserts that researchers can judge the importance, the significance, of a theme in specific discrete quanta of content by the amount of space it occupies.

Sampling stochastic source material.

Human communication is stochastic, in that it combines the predictable and the unpredictable. Given a sufficient quantity of source material, however, the researcher can find ways to extract "signal" from "noise." For example, a Harvard graduate student, Ian Lamont, used the open source content analysis program Yoshikoder to analyze thousands of press releases from the New China News Agency (NCNA), the official Chinese state media. He created a custom dictionary that flagged references to the Soviet Union, to Vietnam, and to other regional powers. He then reviewed samples of the flagged sentence fragments to determine whether the context was positive or negative. "Rigorous sampling methods and analysis can minimize researcher bias at the hypothesis and data collection stages," Lamont wrote (2008). He began by taking

> . . . a random sample of 21 NCNA news items from 1977 to 1993 and saving them into a single text file, where they could be subjected to Yoshikoder's word count function. A manual review of the resulting list of words identified hundreds of positive and negative terms and variations. These were copied and pasted into two separate text files that became the NCNA negative and positive dictionaries. (2008)

This study of Nutuk is working with a smaller set of documents, and therefore studied all the individual words used in order to have a sufficiently large "sample size" to support valid observations.

Reliability.

Replicability is one of the advantages of using computerized content analysis. Any researcher who uses the same software and the same dictionary on the same source documents will experience the same results. This approach is reliable. The Yoshikoder dictionary is a straightforward XML file, an ASCII text document that can be read and edited with almost any word processor. This is a "white box" approach to data processing and manipulation, with the operations open and visible to the evaluation of other researchers. This study embraces the "open source" perspective, and eschews proprietary, "black box" solutions. The results, and the steps taken to achieve those results, are all open to inspection. You can evaluate the conclusions this chapter reaches with confidence, since the process of reaching them is transparent. The validity of the process is supported by the open source aphorism, "Given a sufficient number of eyeballs, all bugs are visible."

The goal of this study is to isolate and analyze valuable insights from Nutuk, as compared to Augustine's masterpiece and as contrasted against Plato's Republic.

Unitizing and coding: Ἐν ἀρχῃ ἠν ὁ Λογοσ[3].

Units of measurement in content analysis can be articles, songs, speeches, or chapters. For a more fine-grained approach, when doing qualitative research, the researcher can analyze and catalogue individual sentences or clauses in the documents studied.

For this project, which uses an automated dictionary-based approach, the unit of measurement is the word. The assumption is that writers or speakers will write or speak more frequently of things they consider to be of greater significance. Word choice is especially interesting in cases where the judgment of history confirms that the document being studied achieved extraordinary results.

Dictionaries and barking about barking.

Positivism asserts that almost anything can be objectively assessed. Science consists of measuring, weighing, and counting the components of reality. By mastering the little picture, we come to understand the big picture. The lab experiment illuminates the universe; the same force tugs on the moon and on the apple.

Content analysis converts words into numbers, teases insights out of the numbers using mathematical operations, and then translates the results back into words. But should we "operationalize" and count the words themselves? The concepts that the words represent? The physical appearance of the words? Or the labels we assign to the words?

"A dog can bark but he can't bark a tract on barking," Kenneth Burke wrote (Burke, 2003, p. 141). Creating metalanguages, languages about language, is a uniquely human

---

[3] "In the beginning was the Word." John's Gospel, 1:1.

trait. When we discuss languages, we can describe the appearance of the tokens, or we can apply labels that describe the meanings of selected discrete quanta. When we analyze a landmark in literature, we are talking about talking, barking about barking. We talk about what the original writer or speaker talked about, erecting the scaffold of a metalanguage around the language we meet in the speech, book, or other communication artifact. We then pull away from the surface of the artifact, in order to get a better look at the major features, which can be lost in the mass of details. Content analysis, whether done by hand or with the aid of software, allows us to see the forest as well as the trees.

Digital metalanguages.

A blue-collar metalanguage appeared within recent decades, as the needs of the publishing industry drove the creation of Structured Generalized Markup Language (SGML). This protocol for embedding non-printing tokens within the text of a document controls the way a computerized printing press formats the finished product (Vint, 1999).

Tim Berners-Lee drew upon this resource to develop hypertext markup language (HTML). He subtracted all but the most rudimentary formatting features, and added links. When the dust settled and graphical browsers appeared, the World Wide Web, the global Internet, appeared as well (Downing & Fox, 1995).

A more recent development in the field of information management is the eXtensible Markup Language (XML), which permits the user to "tag" chunks of text with labels that reflect their content as well as their appearance. The power of XML is its flexibility. People who are willing to follow a few industry standards can create their own data dictionaries, their own suites of labels structured in their own idiomatic hierarchies (Pardi, 1999).

John Wilkins, Ramon Lull.

The concept of tagging chunks of text, then operating algebraically upon the labels, did not spring full-grown from the forehead of our generation. Arika Okrent's study of invented languages takes us back to the 17th century, when mathematics acquired universally recognized signs for such operations as addition, subtraction, multiplication, division, and square roots. It was suddenly possible to describe actions in a wordless way that was nonetheless understandable throughout Europe. Commercial contacts with the Middle Kingdom, China, made European savants aware of a pictographic written language that could be understood by speakers of hundreds of mutually incomprehensible dialects. Surely, the curse of Babel could now be reversed! (Okrent, 2009).

One scholar who stepped up to this challenge, John Wilkins, wished to create the language that would make it possible to communicate scientific advances with a precision not found in unruly, ambiguous, natural languages (Okrent, 2009, pp. 26-73). Even as Orwell's "newspeak" was designed to make treasonous thought impossible (Orwell, 1977, p. 52), Wilkins' new "philosophical" language forced writers and speakers to write or say exactly what they meant, with no room for misunderstanding. In the first thesaurus of the English language, Wilkins mapped out how, in many cases, numerous English words could be replaced by just one of his.

His project ended with him.

Wilkins' efforts to impose mathematical rigor upon human discourse was presaged more than four centuries earlier by Ramon Llull (Johnston, 1987). Like Wilkins, Llull developed an algebra of language, assigning tags to specific concepts. His *Ars Generalis Ultima* or *Ars Magna* (Great Art of Everything) allowed the master of his encoding process to mechanically combine existing philosophical concepts in new ways, so as to develop new ideas.

But the question remains, what is the best way to "tokenize" something as complex as a living language, so that the metalanguage can be analyzed for clues as to the intent of the original text? A metaphor may be the best way to reason our way forward on this point.

Μη θησαυριζετε 'υμιν θησαυρπους[4] (Matt. 6:19):

Compare a living human language to a hologram. A language, like a hologram, is a massively redundant tool for managing information. If you shine a beam of coherent light through a hologram, a three-dimensional image appears to float in midair. Cut the hologram in half. Shine a laser through it again. The complete original image will reappear, with slightly less resolution. This process can be repeated time after time, with the same result.

A language, like a hologram, can undergo serious reductions yet continue to function. In some contexts, excess vocabulary is even a handicap. To make an invented language work, the inventor needs to find a way to eliminate the messy ambiguity of natural languages. To purge synonyms from his scientific language, Wilkins invented the thesaurus – then used it in exactly the opposite way from that used by most aspiring writers today. In Wilkins' system, many clusters of English

---

[4] Do not treasure up for yourselves treasures … this one sentence uses both the noun and verb forms of the Greek word that became the English *thesaurus*. Much content analysis uses an anti-thesaurus approach, to restrict, rather than expand, the vocabulary you are dealing with.

words, synonyms, and euphemisms including "Sir Reverence" (Okrent, 2009, p. 56) could be replaced with a single word from his philosophical language.

Charles K. Ogden replicated this feat in a more practical way in the early 20th century, creating an artificial language named after the leading empires of his day, British, American, Scientific, Industrial and Commercial – BASIC English (Verduijn, 2004, p. 43). He asserted that a carefully-chosen 850 word vocabulary could be used to express any thought, even though "large sweet round vegetable" takes more time to say than "watermelon." Even with a few technical terms added, BASIC English vocabularies typically contain fewer than a thousand words.

Time has validated the commercial value of Ogden's insight. Several restricted grammar/controlled vocabulary commercial language subsets of English have been implemented since then. By 1985, a year after the title of Orwell's book that introduced "newspeak" to the vernacular, a consortium of European aerospace firms created AECMA Simplified English. The writer who followed these guidelines used fewer than 1,000 words, governed by 60 rules, to precisely and clearly specify the manufacture and maintenance of high-stakes aeronautical hardware. The core of the system was a "reverse thesaurus" that listed ambiguous words, and specified permitted alternatives. Instead of "want," use "BE NECESSARY." Instead of the verb "crop," the writer is required to use CUT or REMOVE (AECMA, 1989, p. 3-1-C28).

The Caterpillar Company, maker of heavy equipment with worldwide distribution, created Caterpillar Fundamental English (CFE) in 1970 as the language of choice for its repair and maintenance manuals. With a restricted vocabulary of around 1,000 words and a carefully chosen permitted set of syntax constructions, CFE could be mastered in less than a month of study (Verduijn, 2004, pp. 45-47).

Peaceful commerce and bruising collisions with widely varied cultures around the globe and across the centuries endowed English with one of the largest vocabularies of all the world's languages. In a process similar to cutting holograph film, a careful linguist can funnel a half-million words down through the bottleneck of a thousand permitted words, and still have a completely functional language.

It is then possible to take this process a step or more further to generate a subset of the language, suitable for expressing specific themes. Computer software can do this automatically and nearly instantly, using a pre-defined "dictionary" to wage war on synonyms. For example, the Linguistic Inquiry and Word Count (LIWC) dictionary reduces a 50,000 word English dictionary to 72 categories, and those to 11 themes.

The redundancy found in any normal human language supports the validity of using data dictionaries to abstract a handful of themes from documents that use tens of thousands of different words. There is so much "overkill" in the source material that a good automated system can refine matching handfuls of radium from two different piles of pitchblende. It is this redundancy, this lavish use of synonyms, which makes the process practical. If normal human languages were not so redundant, not so rife with alternate channels and backup systems, then it would be impossible to compare a document written in one language to a document written in another. Christians would need to learn Greek, Hebrew, and Aramaic before daring to open their Bibles, even as Muslims insist that only the Arabic Qur'an is legitimate.

It is true that the City was written in classical Latin, and Nutuk in archaic Turkish. However, even a scholar who mastered both languages, and did all the translating personally, could not have an equal facility in both languages. A more pragmatic approach is to rely upon the competence and good faith of those who translated these source documents into English, and upon the superfluity of expressiveness found in English, Latin, Turkish, and any other natural language. If our expectations are modest, the inherent robust redundancy of natural languages makes it possible to extract interesting and helpful, if not conclusive, information from translated documents.

Specifications for this Study

Rationale for selecting Yoshikoder.

Neuendorf (2004) posted a list of Computer Content Analysis Programs that summarized the available field of candidates. This list grouped the software as quantitative programs, qualitative programs, miscellaneous text-analysis programs, and video analysis programs. Many of these programs are commercial software. Some are free, some are open-source and free. One commercial program, Diction 5.0, comes with proprietary built-in "black box" dictionaries to analyze five targeted semantic features – Activity, Optimism, Certainty, Realism, and Commonality – plus an additional 35 sub-features. However, the user does not have access to the inner logic of the dictionaries.

Dictionary-based programs perform "the basic handful" of functions: word frequency counts and analysis, category frequency counts and analysis, and visualization. Normally, programs that count words can also "lemmatize" them, to aggregate words with the same root in varied inflections. They also bunch synonyms together. A category frequency analysis function assigns categories of words to single labels. The Linguistic Inquiry and Word Count (LIWC) dictionary, for example, boasts a category 59 (death) that covers all the ways this event can happen, and be processed by the survivors. Visualization permits the researcher to see how frequently and how closely concepts flock together.

A working paper by Christina Silver and Ann Lewis, *Choosing a CAQDAS Package*, provided an overview of the software available to aid with qualitative content analysis, and a description of the leading contenders in the field. These scholars do not have many recommendations for those pursuing a more quantitative path.

The article "Text Analysis Info – Content: quantitative with category system" evaluated the software available, as of September 2008, for quantitative content analysis. It begins with CoAn2.08, a Windows program based on Intext. This program has many notable features, but is only available in a German-language edition.

Given the academic imperatives of openness and replicability, the best tool for the job of comparing the documents in this study was Yoshikoder, an open-source program that supports a "white box" model, where every step is visible. Several other factors made Yoshikoder the best of the breed for the purpose of this dissertation. It can accept input in ASCII, Unicode (UTF-8), or Asian encodings. It provides summaries and comparisons of documents, in addition to the standard quantitative measures. The researcher can use RID and LIWC dictionaries that have been adapted to the XML format. Since legitimate XML files can be read and edited by generic text editors, researchers can also easily adapt or create their own customized dictionaries.

Document selection and preparation.

The primary document examined, Nutuk, was downloaded from a web site using a Python script. The documents it was compared against, Augustine's City and Plato's Republic, were retrieved from the Project Gutenberg online public domain library as ASCII text files. These documents were lightly edited to remove the introductions, prefaces, footnotes, and other extraneous material. By comparing Nutuk to one good example of world-changing literature, a gold standard, and again to a sterile fantasy, an iron pyrite standard, this study extracted insights about powerful rhetorical elements in this overlooked and understudied historical monument. We placed ourselves in an optometrist's chair, projected Nutuk against the wall, and viewed this document through contrasting lenses and filters to help some of the elements that contributed to its rhetorical power snap into sharp focus.

Using existing dictionaries.

Could existing dictionaries be used to highlight the common elements shared by Nutuk and City, while distinguishing them from the speculative literature? A simple preliminary test was quickly performed, analyzing these documents using two standard dictionaries. A dictionary report was generated that provided a list of the words and word categories, the frequency with which each word or word family was used in each document, and a proportion value that compared the count of each word or word family to the document's total word count. The dictionary reports were exported to Microsoft Excel .xls files, then opened using Open Office, the open-source equivalent to the MS Office suite. The numeric outputs were then selected, and checked for correlation.

Initial results were disappointing. The three documents in question all displayed high correlation with each other when compared against the LIWC dictionary, and low when compared against the Laval-Garry dictionary. It appears that the existing dictionaries were not appropriate tools to help us understand what makes Nutuk similar to City and unlike

Republic. The choices were, to go back to square one and choose a different software tool, or to find a better dictionary for Yoshikoder. A better dictionary would generate results that demonstrate high correlation in the desired quadrant, and low on the seamy side of the tracks. At this point, a review of Lamont's experience made clear how straightforward it is to make a customized dictionary.

Creating a new dictionary.

In his study of Chinese media, Lamont created simple dictionaries that looked for a mere handful of terms. He then used the concordance function of Yoshikoder to evaluate these terms in context, and counted up the number of positive versus negative associations with each term. These became the basis for two new dictionaries, which generated the numbers he used to support his thesis that the Chinese leaders were more concerned about the influence Vietnam exercised in the region than they were about the strong ties between Hanoi and Moscow.

To create a dictionary, the Yoshikoder user selects the target words, groups them into appropriate categories, and then adds the XML tags.

Encouraged by Lamont's approach, I began by using Yoshikoder to create lists of all the words found in the three primary documents, and the frequencies of each word's usage. I examined the word count and word frequency lists generated by this software in order to develop a Yoshikoder "dictionary" that focused attention on the elements that Nutuk and City have in common, but do not share with the dystopian classic. The word count feature of this software generated a "proportion" field that divided the number of times each word occurs by the total number of words in its document. I exported this report to an Excel spreadsheet, and opened the document in Open Office.

The original word-count output generated by Yoshikoder included 21,314 lines, each of which contained the following information:

Table 1 *Information Included in Word-Count Output Lines*

Word	Count (1)	Count (2)	Count (3)	Prop. (1)	Prop. (2)
Prop. (3)					

The Word field is, of course, the word that the word count feature found. Count (1) provides the number of times the word appeared in Nutuk, Count (2) provides the number of times the word appeared in City, and Count (3) provides the number of times the word appeared in Republic. Prop. (1) is the proportion, the count divided by the total number of words in Nutuk. Prop. (2) and Prop. (3) provide the proportions for City and Republic.

A representative line, for the verb "abandon," contained the following information:

Table 2 *Representative Word-Count Output Line*

abandon	35	19	0	0.000106825215634	0.000042997320588
0.000000000000000					

This word appeared 35 times in Nutuk, 19 times in City, and nowhere in Republic.

At this point, we had more than 21,000 words to analyze. Which of these words show up with a frequency that can, perhaps, shed light on the rhetorical power of Nutuk? How do we sift out the wheat from the chaff? How do we isolate the words of interest, in order to subject them to closer scrutiny?

First attempt

A first attempt to winnow the words used the raw word counts. Since the documents have a different number of total words, I multiplied each count by a correction factor. Since City has 1.35 times as many words as Nutuk, I used the Open Office Calc spreadsheet to multiply all the word counts in the Nutuk column by 1.35. These lines were then sorted by the size of the word count, from largest to smallest (City field), then from largest to smallest (Nutuk field), then finally alphabetically. I visually compared the adjusted word counts, to include those that occurred with approximately equal frequency in Nutuk and City, give or take 50%, and to exclude those that occurred with approximately equal frequency in Republic. After a great deal of work with highlighters and hard copy, I zeroed in on 17 interesting words for further consideration.

A more rigorous attempt

Although this approach yielded some intriguing results, the lack of replicable rigor suggested that there had to be a better way. Using the proportion fields would eliminate the need for a correction factor, and permit more precise comparisons. However, the researcher would be working with very small numbers, with too many decimal places. The proportion values looked much like absurdly tiny linguistic farads.[5]

Since the goal is to analyze Nutuk, a quick slice with Occam's razor eliminated all the words that did not appear in Atatürk's

---

[5] The farad, which measures the electrical value of capacitance, is one of the strangest standard units of measurement in common use. There is very little market demand for ten farad capacitors. The more typical sizes are measured in millionths, billionths or trillionths of a farad: microfarads (μF or MFD), nanofarads (nF), or picofarads (pF). When expressed as ratios, numbers can get very small, indeed.

masterwork. This reduced the word count by half. The quest then began to isolate the words that occurred with approximately equal frequency in Nutuk and City by using automated techniques. Could a Structured Query Language (SQL) command compare word frequency proportions in one document to those that appeared in another, give or take a preset range?

The first step was to convert the Excel spreadsheet into an Open Office database. Although the Open Office database does support some SQL functionality, attempts to create a query that compared Value A to Value B +/- 50% failed to generate the desired results. Open Office SQL did not facilitate the comparison of a given value to a computed set of values.

There are other ways, however, to create approximations, if you find yourself unable to do an on-the-fly calculation as a program runs. Why not pre-screen the data, before feeding it into Yoshikoder? A new look at the spreadsheet suggested a useful approach. Each proportion field was multiplied by 1,000 and then the part of each number to the right of the decimal point was truncated to two places. This made it possible to match words with a permitted variation of +/- 0.5%. I converted the revised spreadsheet into an Open Office database, and developed a simple SQL query:

```
SELECT * FROM "oct28c" WHERE "Nutuk" = "City"
AND NOT "Nutuk" = "Republic"
AND  "Nutuk" > 0.01
```

This script extracted records that included words, and their associated numeric values, that occurred with nearly equal frequency in Nutuk and City. The script then filtered out words that either occurred with equal frequency in Republic, or failed to clear a threshold value. This query generated 144 interesting words. If the query were changed to exclude words with an adjusted frequency of at least 0.02, the result was 68 words. If the frequency value was set to 0.03, the result was 49 words. I decided to go with the larger number.

When all of the 144 selected words were examined using the correlation function of Open Office Calc, the results indicated a correlation of 1 between Nutuk and City. Since the SQL script only selected words that occurred with nearly equal frequency in Nutuk and City, by definition they will always have a correlation of 1. The correlation between Nutuk and Republic, on the other hand, was 0.6. This was unacceptable, since it indicated that a comparison of the full range of selected words failed to sufficiently distinguish between these two documents.

At this point, the concept of *overhead* comes into play. Any natural language includes a certain amount of overhead, function words that organize the structure of a message. A helpful comparison is the Internet Protocol version 4 (IPv4) packet. Each discrete quanta of information is comprised of "header" and "data" parts. Before a network-attached device can get to the data, it needs to wade through 12 or 13 fields of information about the length of the data field, where the packet came from, where it is going, and what format it is in. It seemed reasonable to assume that the highest-correlation words were "header" material, too common to provide a useful tool for distinguishing between Nutuk and Republic. By repeatedly measuring correlation over a variety of ranges, it was determined that the best and clearest results could be obtained from measuring the bottom 81 values, which yielded a correlation of -0.02.

The 81 words that survived this sifting process were:

Table 3 *Final Group of Words Selected for Comparison*

absence	accomplish	accurately	acquainted	acquired
adapted	addressing	afforded	attainment	beforehand
bloodshed	certainty	changing	closed	communities	complain
confident	confirm	contradict	contribute	convicted	cruelties
cry	customs	deceiving	deemed	dependent	differ
enlightened	evidently	exceed	excuse	expresses	fitting
governing	increasing	inflict	lacking	lasting	lastly	medical
method	moderate	murdered	native	obtaining	originally
path	patriarch	permanent	persist	popular	practice
preference	prefers	preservation	preserving	presumption
prime	promising	punish	recent	reminded	rendering
requisite	resisted	sides	so-called	soil	solid	sooner	spend
spring	terminated	therein	threw	thrown	touched	treasure
treatment	warned	withdrawn	yourselves

The next step was to visually examine these key words, to see if any categories were immediately apparent. Ten major themes initially seemed to make sense: *secure, enduring, true, false, achievement, means, relational, choice, deficient,* and *time.* However, when the selected 81 words were grouped into the first-glance ten categories, and the correlations measured, an immediate need for improvement appeared. Some of the categories demonstrated a negative correlation between the Nutuk and Republic word groupings, which was what we sought. Approximately half of the categories, however, either had a positive correlation, or simply refused to compute, generating the #DIV/0 error message.

After a lengthy heuristic process of repeatedly re-grouping the key words and retesting for correlation, it was possible to create a dictionary that grouped these words into five major valid categories. Intriguingly enough, the five categories that the statistical software indicated best summarized the distinguishing words of Nutuk were very similar to the five points of the model treaty discussed in the last chapter. There were no more #DIV/0 error messages.

The table below depicts the successful categories, and the words assigned to each category:

Table 4 *Successful Categories and Contents*

Category	Contents
Transcendence	accurately certainty confident confirm contradict enlightened evidently fitting lasting permanent persist preservation preserving presumption resisted sides soil solid treasure
Hierarchy / Community	acquainted addressing communities contribute customs medical native patriarch promising rendering therein touched treatment withdrawn yourselves
Ethics	absence adapted afforded bloodshed changing complain cruelties cry deceiving dependent exceed excuse increasing inflict lacking method murdered obtaining path practice prime so-called spend
Oath / Treaty	convicted deemed differ expresses governing popular preference prefers punish reminded requisite warned
Succession / Time	accomplish acquired attainment beforehand closed lastly originally recent sooner terminated threw thrown

Analysis

We have the same attribute

Transcendence had a correspondence of 0 between Nutuk and Republic. The hierarchy/community correlation was -0.23. The ethics category demonstrated a weak correlation of 0.49, which was interesting, but not convincing. The oath/treaty category had a correlation of -0.22. The succession/time category had a correlation of -0.41. As the figure below demonstrates, according to this dictionary, Nutuk and Republic belong to strikingly different genres. Both agree, somewhat, on the desirability of ethical behavior. However, there is no shared level of interest in transcendent matters. Republic also displays pronounced, if varying, degrees of antithesis to the Nutuk concerns about hierarchy, treaty obligations, and time.

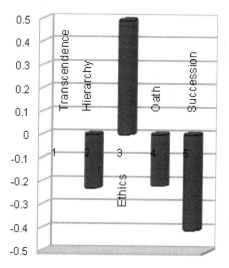

Figure 1. Representation of category correlations between Nutuk and Republic.

Further analysis revealed a similar allocation of emphases to the five categories in Nutuk and City. As the three pie charts below indicate, Nutuk and City belong to the same genre. Republic is a different kind of document, with a different agenda:

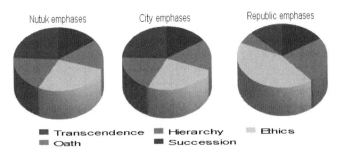

Figure 2. Comparison of emphases allocation between Nutuk,
City, and Republic.

These values can be represented in tabular form, to indicate
the percentage of dictionary hits that fell into each category:

Table 5   *Percentage of Dictionary Hits per Category for Nutuk,
City, and Republic*

Dictionary Categories	Nutuk		City		Republic	
	Word Count	%age	Word Count	%age	Word Count	%age
Transcendence	126	0.24%	180	0.24%	22	0.12%
Hierarchy	98	0.19%	138	0.19%	11	0.06%
Ethics	145	0.27%	194	0.26%	78	0.43%
Oath	80	0.15%	115	0.15%	42	0.23%
Succession	79	0.15%	115	0.15%	29	0.16%

Once again, it is remarkable to note how the two commended
documents assign similar percentages of emphasis to each of
the categories.

Dancing attendance in the penumbra

We now had a dictionary that could be applied to Nutuk and City in order to examine some of the common emphases that made these works effective, and marked them as members of the same genre. However, it would also be useful to examine the ways in which these documents contrasted with each other. We needed to examine the words that occurred most frequently in the neighborhood of each dictionary word.

The next step was to create ten concordances, one for each category in Nutuk and in City. Each concordance displayed the selected key word each time it occurred in the document, and six words on either side of that key word. It is possible, but was not productive, to reiterate the process and use Yoshikoder to create word frequency reports based on concordance reports. However, a few dozen concordance entries would then become a few hundred lines in a spreadsheet, with the words listed alphabetically, and the context lost.

A more visual approach to representing the word families that flocked around each major dictionary category seemed appropriate. A text block comprising all the words in each concordance was then processed through the "Wordle" program found at http://www.wordle.net to generate a graphic depiction of significant verbiage. Visual examination of each graphic let me isolate prominent words in each concordance that were not shared. It was then possible to evaluate the congruencies and the contrasts of these two documents.

Transcendence/historical prologue

The following words received equal emphasis, appearing with nearly equal frequency, in both Nutuk and City.

Table 6 *Transcendence/Historical Words Receiving Equal Emphasis in Nutuk and City*

Category	Contents
Transcendence	accurately certainty confident confirm contradict enlightened evidently fitting lasting permanent persist preservation preserving presumption resisted sides soil solid treasure

To see which other words received emphasis in these two documents, we used Wordle to create a graphic representation of linguistic attention. The illustration below is the Wordle diagram for Nutuk:

Figure 3. Wordle diagram of transcendence/historical words in Nutuk.

Words considered worthy of attention by the Wordle software, that were *not* found in the project dictionary, were: national, cabinet, nation, question, independence, caliphate, Bey, attack.

The illustration below displays the Wordle diagram for City:

Figure 4. Wordle diagram of transcendence/historical words in City.

Words highlighted by the Wordle software that were *not* found in the project dictionary were: men, things, god, man, eternal, good, away, body, rather, speak, many, miracles, nothing, therefore.

The table below illustrates the frequency of these non-dictionary words:

Table 7 *Frequency of transcendence/historical non-dictionary words in Nutuk and City*

Nutuk	#	City	#
National	9	Men	17
Cabinet	8	Things	12
Nation	8	God	9
Question	6	Man	7
Independence	6	Eternal	6
Caliphate	5	Good	6
Bey	5	Away	5
Attack	5	Body	5
Immediately	4	Rather	5
		Speak	5

Nutuk	#	City	#
		Many	4
		miracles	4
		Nothing	4
		Therefore	4

These results seem to indicate that Atatürk's transcendence was of a this-worldly variety, with a focus on national identity, challenges to that identity, and the roles of the official players in the drama. The Turkish word *Bey* is a title of respect, analogous to the English Sir or Mister. Atatürk used it primarily when referring to people who held official positions.

Augustine was speaking to humanity, about concrete things, as seen in the light of the eternal God. The words Man and Men occur 24 times in the concordance created to study the use of Transcendence words in City.

Hierarchy/community

The following words received equal emphasis, appearing with nearly equal frequency, in both Nutuk and City.

Table 8 *Hierarchy/Community Words Receiving Equal Emphasis in Nutuk and City*

Category	Contents
Hierarchy / community	acquainted addressing communities contribute customs medical native patriarch promising rendering therein touched treatment withdrawn yourselves

The illustration below displays the Wordle diagram for Nutuk:

Figure 5. Wordle diagram of hierarchy/community words in Nutuk.

Words highlighted by the Wordle software that were not found in the project dictionary were: Bey, well, therein, question, Constantinople, states, fate, idea, officers, Mohamedan, salvation, factors, declared, chose.

The illustration below displays the Wordle diagram for City:

Figure 6. Wordle diagram of hierarchy/community words in City.

Words highlighted by the Wordle software that were not found in the project dictionary were: men, God, even, might, though, book, great, made, neither, number, laws, another, things.

The table below illustrates the frequency of these non-dictionary words:

Table 9 *Frequency of Hierarchy/Community Non-Dictionary Words in Nutuk and City*

Nutuk	#	City	#
Bey	8	Men	22
Well	7	God	11
Therein	6	Even	9
Question	6	Might	7
Constantinople	4	Though	7
States	3	Book	6
Fate	3	Great	5
Idea	3	Made	5
Officers	3	Neither	5
Mohamedan	3	Number	5
Salvation	2	Laws	4
Factors	2	Another	3
Declared	2	Things	3
Chose	2		

These results seem to indicate that Atatürk's hierarchy was a political embodiment and implementation of such big-picture words as fate, idea, and salvation. Augustine's hierarchy incorporated a potent, ordered array of God and people, and the written revelation that defined their interrelationships.

Ethics

The following words received equal emphasis, appearing with nearly equal frequency, in both Nutuk and City.

Table 10 *Ethics Words Receiving Equal Emphasis in Nutuk and City*

Category	Contents
Ethics	absence adapted afforded bloodshed changing complain cruelties cry deceiving dependent exceed excuse increasing inflict lacking method murdered obtaining path practice prime so-called spend

The illustration below displays the Wordle diagram for Nutuk:

Figure 7. Wordle diagram for ethics words in Nutuk.

Words highlighted by the Wordle software that were not found in the project dictionary were: Pasha, made, minister, Bey, hand, government, Greek, opportunity, spend, people, affair, Turkish, front, country, protest, resolutions.

The illustration below displays the Wordle diagram for City:

Figure 8. Wordle diagram for ethics words in City.

Words highlighted by the Wordle software that were not found in the project dictionary were: sin, men, one, life, great, let, gods, nature, though, much, righteousness, even, unchangeable, first, following, words, reason.

The table below illustrates the frequency of these non-dictionary words:

Table 11 *Frequency of Ethics Non-Dictionary Words in Nutuk and City*

Nutuk	#	City	#
pasha	10	sin	22
made	8	Men	16
minister	8	One	13
Bey	7	life	13
hand	7	Great	10
government	5	let	9
Greek	5	gods	8
opportunity	5	nature	7
spend	5	Though	7

Nutuk	#	City	#
people	4	much	6
affair	4	righteousness	5
Turkish	4	Even	5
front	4	unchangeable	4
country	3	first	4
protest	3	following	3
resolutions	3	words	3
		reason	3

These results seem to indicate that, for Atatürk, ethics could be defined as that which furthered the interests of his people, and confounded the interests of rival tribes. Augustine was more focused on matters of people and their personal sin and righteousness, in the sight of God and in view of the eternal, unchangeable order.

Oath/judicial

The following words received equal emphasis, appearing with nearly equal frequency, in both Nutuk and City.

Table 12   *Oath/Judicial Words Receiving Equal Emphasis in Nutuk and City*

Category	Contents
Oath / treaty	convicted deemed differ expresses governing popular preference prefers punish reminded requisite warned

The illustration below displays the Wordle diagram for Nutuk:

Figure 9. Wordle diagram of oath/judicial words in Nutuk.

Words highlighted by the Wordle software that were not found in the project dictionary were: certain, treason, necessary, sent, nation, individuals, authority, question, pasha, Cabinet, remain.

The illustration below displays the Wordle diagram for City:

Figure 10. Wordle diagram for oath/judicial words in City.

Words highlighted by the Wordle software that were not found in the project dictionary were: God, one, though, even, things, present, whether, Christ, yet, words, compelled, good, worthy.

The table below illustrates the frequency of these non-dictionary words:

Table 13 *Frequency of Oath/Judicial Non-Dictionary Words in Nutuk and City*

Nutuk	#	City	#
certain	7	God	12
treason	7	One	9
necessary	6	though	8
sent	5	even	8
Nation	5	things	6
individuals	4	present	6
authority	4	whether	5
Question	4	Christ	4
pasha	4	yet	4
Cabinet	3	words	3
remain	3	compelled	3
		good	3
		worthy	3

These results seem to indicate that Atatürk viewed the defining allegiance as to his nation and those who led it. Augustine's first loyalty was to God and Christ, as the cornerstone of just decisions.

Inheritance

The following words received equal emphasis, appearing with nearly equal frequency, in both Nutuk and City.

Table 14 *Inheritance Words Receiving Equal Emphasis in Nutuk and City*

Category	Contents
Succession / time	accomplish acquired attainment beforehand closed lastly originally recent sooner terminated threw thrown

The illustration below displays the Wordle diagram for Nutuk:

Figure 11. Wordle diagram of inheritance words in Nutuk.

Words highlighted by the Wordle software that were not found in the project dictionary were: lastly, later, certain, events, originally, political, sons, country, independence, assembly, relation, party, position, taken, may, national, account.

The illustration below displays the Wordle diagram for City:

Figure 12. Wordle diagram of inheritance words in City.

Words highlighted by the Wordle software that were not found in the project dictionary were: one, war, good, man, may, open, Rome, things, gates, gods, reputation, nothing, created, cruelly, help, true.

The table below illustrates the frequency of these non-dictionary words:

Table 15 *Frequency of Inheritance Non-Dictionary Words in Nutuk and City*

Nutuk	#	City	#
lastly	8	one	17
later	8	war	10
certain	6	good	8
events	5	man	6
originally	5	may	5
political	5	open	5
sons	5	Rome	4
country	4	things	4

Nutuk	#	City	#
Independence	4	gates	4
assembly	4	gods	3
relation	3	reputation	3
party	3	nothing	3
position	3	created	3
taken	3	cruelly	3
May	3	help	3
National	3	true	3
account	2	yet	3

These results seem to indicate that the end point, the goal, the destination in Atatürk's world view was the nation, whose independence and political integrity were the legacy he would bequeath to the future. Augustine, on the other hand, was aware of both the underlying unity of the city of God, and of the incessant cruel warfare against it. The future might be good, but it would also be demanding.

When we examine the merged non-dictionary word frequencies for all of the dictionary categories, the cumulative results reinforce the impression that Augustine and Atatürk had different ultimate concerns. The table below lists the words that appeared in two or more of the five dictionary categories, suggesting they were key elements of the world views of these world shapers:

Table 16 *Words Appearing in Two or More Dictionary Categories*

Nutuk	Number of occurrences	City	Number of occurrences
nation + national + independence + country	36	men	55
question	16	one	39
cabinet	15	God	32
pasha	14	things	25
certain	13	though	22
nation	13	even	22
independence	10		
country	7		
national	6		

Life, to Atatürk, was a question to be answered, a challenge to be faced, concerning the nation and its independence. If we add nation, independence, country, and national, we find that these words were used, in conjunction with the dictionary terms, 36 times in our concordances.

The frequent use of words like "though" and "even" suggests that Augustine sought to deal with a nuanced and balanced understanding of God, people, and things.

Quantifiable conclusion

The protagonist of Thornton Wilder's poignant novel *The Bridge of San Luis Rey* believed that theology could be an exact science, and that theodicy could be expressed with a numerical precision analogous to that which characterizes physics. In the final analysis, however, this friar's ambitious purpose came to naught:

> Yet for all his diligence Brother Juniper never knew the central passion of Dona Maria's life; nor of Uncle Pio's, not even of Esteban's. And I, who claim to know so much more, isn't it possible that even I have missed the very spring within the spring? (Wilder, 2004, p. 9)

Content analysis, even when aided by sophisticated computer software, provides modest results, indicators, and suggestions rather than dogmatic pronouncements. Still, if this caveat is kept in mind, the results add incrementally to the available insights concerning the topic of study. This study seems to indicate that the "five-point covenant" paradigm has empirical support as a tool for evaluating communication artifacts. Two very effective documents, in different eras, crafted by very different leaders, and governed by two different religious perspectives, gave nearly identical weights to the categories of the five-point paradigm.

Chapter 5: Conclusions

Rabble-rousers and World-changers

We have evaluated two major works, one well known, and the other deserving of far more recognition, as handbooks for reorganizing broken worlds. *Nutuk* and *City of God* are "diagnostic and repair manuals" for ailing, failing social orders. The explanations Atatürk and Augustine offered their readers made sense to them, provided blueprints for isolating the broken components of their worlds, and recommended newer, better, and more reliable parts. The historical results justified the accuracy of the diagnoses.

"Thou shalt not follow a multitude to do evil," Moses admonished his hearers in Exodus 23:2. During eras of social catastrophe, mountebanks and charlatans find it easier to gain a hearing. In the immediate aftermath of the Protestant Reformation, the "black hundreds" of the Peasant Rebellion marched through central Europe with their menacing, egalitarian chant:

> When Adam delved and Eva span, *Kyrie eleison,*
> Where then was the Gentleman, *Kyrie eleison.*

Genteel hierarchies tremble during times of unrest. In 1533-1535, John of Leyden and the Anabaptists brought apocalyptic hysteria to Münster, along with the community of goods and of wives. They considered themselves to be the vanguard of the revolution, the elect theocratic rulers of the earth. They were wrong, but many people died.

During the 1840s, a low-level civil servant who repeatedly failed his Mandarin exams received visions of heaven, a golden-bearded God the Father, Jesus, and the heavenly harem of the Son of God. He also learned that he, Hong, was

God's Chinese Son, appointed agent for an Asian millennial era. Twenty million corpses later, history delivered a different verdict (Spence, 1996).

Charles G. Finney embodied a great deal of the independent, brash, confident spirit of the homespun era that shaped the American frontier in the aftermath of the Revolutionary War. His preaching resonated with his audience, and stirred up a great deal of excitement in western New York shortly before Hong's project took off, but *A Shopkeeper's Millennium* failed to materialize (Johnson, 1978). The frantic, militant, self-absorbed self-righteousness Finney preached as his gospel found outlets in a variety of do-gooder crusades, such as vegetarianism, violent abolitionism, the "temperance" movement, the Church of Jesus Christ of Latter-Day Saints, and, perhaps ultimately, the American Civil War.

The "Jesus Freaks" of 1970 America thought they were on the verge of catalyzing major societal transformations. Four decades later, their cultural influence is primarily found inside the walls of fundamentalist megachurches, with services modeled on rock concerts. Choirs, organs, and hymnals are gone. A lead singer croons into a microphone on stage in front, surrounded by shapely, shimmying backup vocalists, and accompanied by an amplified guitar/drums rock combo.

What makes the difference between a movement that has enduring, long-term results, and spasmodic, ephemeral fads? In his epic novel *Les Miserables*, Victor Hugo reflected on the difference between redemptive revolution and *émeute* (pointless civil disturbance):

> The clash of passions and of ignorances is different from the shock of progress. Rise if you will, but to grow. Show me to which side you are going. There is no insurrection but forward. Every other rising is evil, every violent step

backwards is an émeute: to retreat is an act of violence against the human race. Insurrection is the Truth's access of fury: the paving stones which insurrection tears up throw off the spark of right. These stones leave to the émeute only their mud. Danton against Louis XVI is insurrection. Hebert against Danton is émeute.

Hence it is that if insurrection in given cases may be as Lafayette said the most sacred of duties, an émeute may be the most deadly of crimes.

There is also some difference in the intensity of caloric: the insurrection is often a volcano, the émeute is often a fire of straw. (Hugo, 1889, p. 127)

Violent rebellion against civil authority is an ugly affair, Hugo seems to be telling us, that can, sometimes, be justified. There are legitimate rebellions, and there are heinous riots. One event transforms the social landscape. The other is swallowed up by the smug status quo, which then goes on its way as before, with, perhaps, a brief case of cultural indigestion.

If you find yourself inside a mass movement, how can you tell the difference? Will the world be transformed for the better by the songs you sing and the signs you wave? Or will The Powers That Be merely chuckle, and pursue their own agenda with more self-assured verve than ever?

Changing the world takes more than passion, energy, and a violent distaste for the status quo. What can we learn from the lives of those who actually did redefine their worlds? When we summarize the insights extracted from the work of Augustine and Atatürk, what recommendations emerge?

Recommendations for World-changers

If the soul is darkened

By a fear it cannot name,

If the mind is baffled

When the rules don't fit the game,

Who will answer? Who will answer? Who will answer?
(Ames, 1968)

As Berger and Luckmann pointed out, the human habit is to "reify" the status quo, to assume that the way things are is the way they should be, always have been, and always will be. Languages, and the social orders we create using our languages, normally change very slowly. What do you do, however, when "the rules don't fit the game" any longer? Panic? Yearn for the "good old days"? Or power through to a new definition of collective reality, a new linguistic artifact, a new social order?

How do you build bridges between where your audience is now, and where they need to be? Quite often, you build bridges by asserting: "We are on the wrong track. We need to go back to the point where we got sidetracked, and move forward from there with fresh insights." Atatürk told his people that they were Turks long before they were Ottomans. Before encumbering themselves with the chore of shepherding a motley and ungrateful group of incompatible nations spread over three continents, the Turks enjoyed a valiant, free, and militant life. Augustine reminded his readers that the city of God existed from Adam's day, well before Romulus slew Remus, and that this supernatural intersection of human and divine interests would last long after Rome was dust. Augustine wrote to a society that was predominantly Christian, and exhorted them to value their supernatural and eternal identity over their allegiance to a civil order rooted in paganism.

True reformations are scholarly movements that fully engage the life of the mind. Those who can appeal convincingly to history and the larger contexts of life have a breadth of vision that can only be attained through years of consecrated thought, study, and effort. Enduring social transformations require the most rigorous and focused kind of prolonged mental discipline. Martin Luther was a college professor, an Augustinian monk, before nailing his *Ninety-Five Theses* to the Wittenberg door. John Calvin was a gifted legal student. Even John Wesley, the popularizer of the Reformation, who crafted a mass-market version of the message, was an Oxford graduate who could quote the Greek New Testament from memory more accurately than the English translation. Charles Darwin spent months watching plants grow, and writing voluminously to his devotees. Karl Marx laired in the bowels of the British Museum, and lit the powder train that led to a movement that later ruled a third of the world's people.

As we have seen, Augustine was a scholar and a teacher before he was a Christian, as well as after. He had the best education available to men of his generation, including studies abroad in the academic heart of his civilization. He was conversant with the political, cultural, and religious history of the civilized worlds of his day, both Greek and Roman. His Greek was somewhat limited, but Hellenism was old school by that time, anyhow. When writing for the most sophisticated and responsible readers of his day, Augustine could meet them on their own ground, and quote their own sources.

In like manner, when brilliant young Mustafa broke his mother's heart by seeking a military education rather than a clerical vocation, his intellectual gifts so impressed his teachers that they nicknamed him Kemal – perfection – the name that he adopted as his own years before a grateful nation awarded him the surname held by no one else: Father of the Turks, Atatürk. He was fluent in the language and literature of his own people, and a devotee of French political theorists. Visitors to the Atatürk home, now a museum, can view a copy of *Du contrat social ou Principes du droit politique* – Rousseau's *Social Contract* – with Atatürk's handwritten notes in the margins (Gençer, 2006).

Atatürk was a popular teacher at a military college, and appointed himself schoolmaster to the nation after Turkish independence was achieved. A famous photo of Atatürk shows him at a blackboard in a park teaching a crowd the new Turkish alphabet.

Figure 13. Photograph of Atatürk teaching the new Turkish alphabet.

Nutuk bears evidence of Atatürk's scholarly commitment to primary source material; much of it is composed of the telegraphs he sent and received during the periods described in this speech. He documented his points, and allowed his adversaries to refute themselves with their own words.

170

What else do Augustine and Atatürk have to teach those who seek to work for enduring personal, corporate, or social transformation?

Invoke a Transcendent Purpose

Kline called his first category "historical prologue." When the Great King makes a treaty, he begins by explaining the game-changing events that brought the people to the point where they needed to treat with him, to adapt to the new reality being imposed upon them by cosmic forces beyond their control. One team's side had won, and evidently had the sanction of a clearly-defined ultimate reality. The other team had lost, and needed to get used to it.

Give the bad news first

Like other successful world-changers, Atatürk and Augustine were willing to get their hands dirty serving as the undertakers and gravediggers of the old order. The message that convincing re-imaginers of social reality must communicate is an articulate eulogy that, while recognizing the good things of the departing era, also pronounces the finality of the death sentence over it. The old world is dead. It deserved to die. It embodied fatal flaws, sins, faults, and weaknesses.

When the social order around us is in catastrophic decline, survival trumps tradition. We need to enjoin those around us, "Come out from among her, my people, lest you be partaker of her judgments." Get out while the getting is good. Some things are not worth saving. Some things are beyond saving. Fools only waste precious time and energy if they try to prop up that which is already irreparably broken.

To change the world for a family, client, or community, you need to be able to help your audience see the pointlessness of attempts to redeem the irredeemable. Why emulate the disappointed lovers who carry a torch, for unrewarding lonely years, for the ones who spurned them? To find happiness, one must relinquish that which is lost, and move on.

Then the good news

On the other hand, world-changers need to be able to point to a better way. Augustine invited people to refocus their aspirations on the true Eternal City, the city of God, a city that could not be overthrown, despoiled, or conquered. Treasure in heaven is beyond the reach of rust, moth, and thief. Atatürk challenged his people to get with the program, enter the 20th century, and assume their condign role as a modern nation, a respected peer of other modern, scientific, progressive states.

In 100 words or fewer, what overwhelmingly crucial value can you appeal to? Why should people care about, or even be willing to die for, your cause? Will soldiers cross oceans, leap from trenches, cut through barbed wire, and charge machine gun nests while crying out "For higher Wall Street profits?" (Butler, 2010). Can you articulate your position in a brief core message that resonates with the deepest aspirations of those you address? Although *The City of God* and *Nutuk* were lengthy documents, they were spun out from, and elaborated on, a few key ideas that could be tersely summarized.

For Augustine, the central, energizing concept was *love*. A community is formed by people who agree on the appropriate object of their love. The Christian community is called into being by the proactive love of a creating and redeeming God, and its members show their gratitude by loving human neighbors. Augustine offered those who would listen a sense of eternal security as members of an eternal community, which offered hope for this life and the next.

The key word for Atatürk appears to be *respect*. An imperial people, with a deeply rooted tradition of valor and nobility, had become a joke. The domestic enemies of the Turkish people, the Sultan and his court, were content to serve as domesticated buffoons and comic relief for the nations of the West, running an exotic little theme park/costume ball for the amusement of their captors. This humiliation, Atatürk assured his nation, was not acceptable. Not appropriate. Not suitable for a race of warriors and heroes who had carved out, and maintained, an empire that spanned three continents and more than 800 years. The valor that had made the Turk the terror of Europe could be refocused to create the Turkish Republic – a respected modern nation, a scientific nation, a worthy peer on the world stage with the so-called Great Powers of Europe.

The Sublime Porte offered the Turkish people degradation, humiliation, subjugation. Atatürk assured them that they deserved a better deal. They were worthy of the respect that mattered more to them than life itself – if they would but rally and fight for it.

Forthrightly Identify and Pillory the Villains

Be aware that the old order will always have its defenders. These might be people with a financial stake in the status quo, or a passionate religious commitment to the values that the old way claims to embody. Yet, those who would support a failed or malevolent social order must be exposed as enemies of the good. There are times when politeness is treason. Augustine was unsparing in his denunciations of unsavory Roman leaders and deities. Atatürk had no compassion to spare for the obsolete Oriental despots who were willing to cannibalize their nation in order to protect their own upholstered existence.

Enemies of the common good, traitors to the defining values of the desired social order, must be confronted and named. Would-be leaders who are too reticent, too polite, to call things as they are, can see the movement to which they've given their "lives . . . fortunes, and sacred honor" come to naught. *With Crossed Fingers*, a scholarly account of the subversion of the American Presbyterian Church, concludes that this Protestant denomination was taken over by heterodox elements because the defenders of the orthodox tradition lacked the blunt and forthright candor that Augustine and Atatürk displayed when discussing enemies of their communities. The orthodox Presbyterian leadership were too prissy, too reluctant, too polite, to directly confront the enemies of the sacred tradition entrusted to their care. Pastors and professors were permitted to deny and deride, with impunity, creedal elements that they had sworn in their ordination vows to defend. These "modernist" thought leaders had evidently taken those vows "with crossed fingers," but few responsible parties were willing to take issue with their bad faith. When heterodox forces had accrued enough power to defrock a popular Princeton professor for preaching the virgin birth, North asserts, the loss of this denomination was complete (North, 1996, p. 35).

Atatürk and Augustine's rhetorical efforts show us that those who would work for profound and enduring transformation, on a personal, corporate, or national level, need to be clear, forthright, and unsparing in their declarations about the facts. They need to spell out "who's wearing black hats, and who's wearing white."

Network

Augustine relied upon scribes to hand-copy his work, chapter by chapter, and distribute those copies through couriers traveling on foot, on horseback, and by sailing ship. Atatürk took control of the national telegraph network at an early stage of the Turkish war of liberation, and made effective use of this wired connectivity. Both world-changers used the best means at their disposal to stay in touch with those they sought to influence. To some extent, each worked within the confines of the available media. The components of Augustine's work took longer to produce, longer to distribute, and longer to absorb. Atatürk's work was more "telegraphic" in style, and adapted to the attention spans of a predominantly oral culture. Augustine was responding to a slow-motion train wreck, a "decline and fall" process that spanned decades. Atatürk's telegraphs addressed a society with its back to the wall, in immediate peril, in a literal war for cultural survival.

Effective agents of social transformation view the process as a team sport. They are relentless communicators, and typically maintain a voluminous correspondence. It was not unusual for frontier circuit riding Methodist bishops to write a thousand letters a year (Tipple, 1916, p. 107). The New Testament canon contains a handful of the letters written by a few apostles, the letters that were considered to be worth copying and sharing. Committees of correspondence organized the American revolutionary war.

Ignore this fact of life, and your impact will be minimal. G. K. Chesterton beautifully summarized the grandiose obsession that drives heretics to take their lonely stands and scream defiance at the universe:

> In former days the heretic was proud of not being a heretic. It was the kingdoms of the world and the police and the judges who were heretics. He was orthodox. He had no pride in having rebelled against them; they had rebelled against him. The armies with their cruel security, the kings with their cold faces, the decorous processes of State, the reasonable processes of law – all these like sheep had gone astray. The man was proud of being orthodox, was proud of being right. If he stood alone in a howling wilderness he was

more than a man; he was a church. He was the centre of the
universe; it was round him that the stars swung. (Chesterton,
1919)

Ranting loners do not make history, no matter how passionate
they are. Augustine was clear about his corporate loyalties, to
the Western Catholic church, united by its allegiance to the
Bishop of Rome. He defended the integrity of this spiritual
Rome against both the doctrinal attack of British monk
Pelegius, and the schismatic drives of the Donatists. Pelegius
preached a message much like Charles Finney's, of a graceless
salvation earned through morbid, humorless self-discipline.
The Donatists took issue with the church hierarchy, asserting
that the orthodox bishops had lost their credibility during a
recent period of persecution. Augustine's reply still rings with
his derision for those who would denigrate orthodox
Christianity in order to preen themselves on their superior
piety: "The clouds above proclaim that the Church is rising
everywhere in the world, while frogs grunt from their little
pond: 'Christians? None but us'" (Wills, 1999, p. 78).

Although Abraham Lincoln pioneered the use of the telegraph
as an instrument of leadership in wartime (Wheeler, 2006),
Atatürk used the wired network with unparalleled creativity
and effectiveness. Loyal telegraph operators served as his
intelligence agents in the courts of the Sultan. Atatürk's
proclamations, masterpieces of motivation, were distributed
simultaneously, nation-wide, through this same telegraph
network (Atatürk, 2006, p. 336).

External networking merged with, reinforced, and validated
the results of the internal networking. Atatürk achieved
validation of the Turkish Republic as a bona-fide, full-scale
modern nation by forcing the European powers to treat with
them as one. By repudiating agreements made by illegitimate
interests seeking to harm the Turkish people, and by pursuing

a legitimate negotiated settlement at Lausanne, Atatürk's Turkey established itself as a real player on the world scene.

If you want to change the world, make sure that you and your team stay in touch with each other, and negotiate a consistent interface with the larger world.

Find the Right Ethical Fulcrum

In retrospect, with the wisdom of hindsight, the choices Augustine and Atatürk made were clear. When the barbarians swept through 5th-century Rome, the wise man disconnected his hopes from the sinking ship of pagan bureaucratic Rome, and poured his energies, his attentions into a more enduring social construct, the Christian church. When the Greek soldiers boiled out of Smyrna, spearing towards the Anatolian heartland, the obvious thing to do, in retrospect, was to summon the sons of the soil to defend their turf. Yet, these courses of action were not the only possibilities at the time, nor even, for many observers and participants, the most reasonable. Why not reach some kind of accommodation with the barbarian chieftain, a negotiated reduction in status, a partnership in tax farming, using the Roman bureaucracy already in place? Why not conclude a hasty treaty with the Great Powers of Europe, or even invoke American intervention, to yank on the Hellenic army's leash?

Why not? Well, because the city of God could not be held hostage to political changes of fortune, and still retain its integrity. The Turkish heart and heartland were not, after all, for sale to the highest bidder.

Ethical clarity characterizes influential communicators, but can be hard to find. For example, in the early 1980s, a West Indian preacher addressed an American congregation that embraced the Wesleyan "holiness" tradition. As the world at large vigorously debated the burning issues that inflamed various groups at the beginning of the Reagan presidency, this speaker riveted his audience's attention with a passionate and erudite diatribe against the heinous evil of wearing wedding rings.

We can be stunned by the presumption that compels a charismatic speaker to strain out gnats and swallow camels. Yet, missing the main point is a problem that has bedeviled humanity throughout history. Author C. S. Lewis puts this issue of misplaced emphasis in the mouth of his fictional devil Screwtape:

> The use of Fashions in thought is to distract the attention of men from their real dangers. We direct the fashionable outcry of each generation against those vices of which it is least in danger and fix its approval on the virtue nearest to that vice which we are trying to make endemic. The game is to have them running about with fire extinguishers whenever there is a flood, and all crowding to that side of the boat which is already nearly gunwale under. Thus we make it fashionable to expose the dangers of enthusiasm at the very moment when they are all really becoming worldly and lukewarm; a century later, when we are really making them all Byronic and drunk with emotion, the fashionable outcry is directed against the dangers of the mere "understanding." Cruel ages are put on their guard against Sentimentality, feckless and idle ones against Respectability, lecherous ones against Puritanism . . . (2001, p. 138)

Would-be leaders who focus on the wrong visible symptoms have no enduring impact. In the early 1840s, the issue was the Mexican War. Henry David Thoreau captured the imagination of the American public with his essay on *Civil Disobedience*, a concept later used to powerful effect by Mahatma Gandhi and Martin Luther King, Jr. James R. Lowell supported Thoreau's stand with his hymn *Once To Every Man And Nation*:

> Once to every man and nation,
> comes the moment to decide,
>
> In the strife of truth with falsehood,
> for the good or evil side;
>
> Some great cause, some great decision,
> offering each the bloom or blight,
>
> And the choice goes by forever,
> 'twixt that darkness and that light.
>
> Then to side with truth is noble,
> when we share her wretched crust,
>
> Ere her cause bring fame and profit,
> and 'tis prosperous to be just;
>
> Then it is the brave man chooses
> while the coward stands aside,
>
> Till the multitude make virtue
> of the faith they had denied. (Lowell, 1945)

In the same era, the Methodist Church in the United States struggled with, but could not cohere around, a unified stand on the issue of slavery. The Methodist Church suffered an acrimonious split into northern and southern branches in 1844 (Norwood, 1974, p. 197).

As Douglas Frank demonstrated in his book *Less than Conquerors*, "demon rum" was a convenient surrogate issue for the ravenous and relentless compulsions of the new consumerist society. Billy Sunday was only the most visible exemplar of a broad-based movement to assail the symptom, rather than the disease. He led an organized effort to compel the American public, Christian and non-Christian, to be "holier" than the One who was said to enjoy a good party, the One who made sure that the guests at a wedding feast did not run out of wine. By the time Prohibition was repealed, organized crime was deeply rooted in American society, the public had lost much of its awe for the rule of law, and organized Christian political action was discredited for nearly a century (Frank, 1986, pp. 167-231).

In times of societal distress and chaos, there are many things to complain about, many causes to champion, many small battles that could be fought. And, there are typically one or two major issues that, if tackled head-on, offer the participants some hope of a better day.

Taking the Plunge, Taking the Pledge, Signing up

The ethical dimension of leadership is corporate as well as personal. At some point, those who respond to your message will need to do something visible to publicly eschew the old order and embrace the new. Every social order has its traditions, rituals, and sustaining patterns of behavior. Alcoholics Anonymous gives its members sobriety medals to commemorate weeks, months, and years of being clean and sober. Good little Soviet children were once expected to join the atheistic Young Pioneers. The red scarf was the ticket to career possibilities, and those who eschewed it, such as Baptists, Pentecostals, and Jehovah's Witnesses, consigned themselves to a lifetime of low-income, low-prestige occupations.

To slam the door on the past, Atatürk took severe legal actions against the popular agents of the old order:

> Gentlemen, while the law regarding the Restoration of Order was in force there took place also the closing of the Tekkes, of the convents, and of the mausoleums, as well as the abolition of all sects and all kinds of titles such as Sheikh, Dervish, "Junger," Tschelebi, Occultist, Magician, Mausoleum Guard, etc. (Atatürk, 1985, p. 720)

The older voluntary associations, funded by local people, and led by entrenched figures who had local credibility, had to go. To replace them, Atatürk established "cultural centers" in the villages, to teach reading, science, sanitation, and secular culture. The older network that supported the religious life of the people was co-opted, put on the government payroll. The Turkish state still funds domesticated mosques, and provides the sermons the imams are required to preach therein. The people have places to go, things to do, and people to do them with, in order to declare and sustain their place in the new order. But the doors to the old numinous places are padlocked.

In Augustine's perspective, when people were baptized, they declared their membership in the *City of God*. They turned their backs upon pagan idols, and publicly pledged their allegiance to a Power greater than Caesar. They entered a social order that cohered around this ultimate, higher loyalty. Again, the sacraments provided a visible and recognized demonstration of where their loyalties lay.

To this day, the Turks view military service as a necessary stage in the socialization of their young men. Universal conscription provides one of the largest standing armies in Europe, keeps the borders safe, and maintains the peace in turbulent regions. It also provides a sense of common identity, of membership in a long and honorable tradition.

Christians who, like Augustine, view the kingdom of God and the kingdom of Caesar as separate realms, declare and maintain their sense of separate identity by partaking of the sacraments.

Who Will Inherit?

What kind of bridge to the future can we offer our audience? What kind of future can we direct their attention to? World-changers have reasons for confidence, and an expectation that their perspective will eventually own the field. Present sacrifices are justified by future expectations.

The rebellious Arab village lay in smoking ruins. Ottoman conscripts supplemented their meager pay by looting the pathetic remains. One Turkish officer, impeccably dressed, turned to another and asked, "Do you want to be a man of the past? Or a man of the future?" When his friend cast his vote for the future, Atatürk proclaimed a professionalism and self-respect that eschewed tawdry pillage. Atatürk, a self-proclaimed "man of the future," also believed that a scientific, modern, and rational perspective permitted the True Believer to eventually understand everything, and achieve anything.

Atatürk finished *Nutuk* with a challenge to Turkish youth yet to be born. Augustine traced the anticipated adventure of the *City of God* to the end of time, and beyond. In his book *The Unheavenly City* Edward Banfield explained the defining characteristic of impoverished people: they were, and are, "present-oriented" (1970, p. 275). In the memorable phrase of Hermann Hesse, children of poor families "always need exactly as much as they happen to have" (Hesse, 1968, p. 68).

People with no vision for the future are not likely to have much of a future.

On the other hand, lost futures are also painful facts of life that can clear the way for better hopes.

A persuasive communicator, Aleksandr Solzhenitsyn, documented *The Gulag Archipelago*. Smuggled copies of his books were eagerly read by the Soviet *nomenclatura*, who were then demoralized to discover that they were wrong about the color of their hats. They were history's villains, tawdry evildoers, not the heroic framers and shapers of a glorious new age.

The existentialism and post-modernism spawned by embittered French *philosophes* (Judt, 1992, pp. 16-18) also engendered a "skepticism regarding grand metanarratives." As Özyürek's memorable and poignant book title proclaims, many live today in an atmosphere of *Nostalgia for the Modern*, a sense of loss with nothing in sight to replace the remembered paradise lost.

Science fiction readers who were mentored by such "Golden Age" luminaries as Isaac Asimov, Robert Heinlein, and Arthur C. Clarke mourn the passing of the modern, and resent the loss of their anticipated flying cars and lunar colonies. Modern science had been moving so fast, but then the trajectory went off course. The "cyberpunk" sub-genre of science fiction exuberantly trashed the bright dreams of progress and reveled in the tawdry possibilities of life. Much of the reading public lost interest in possible futures, retreating into the genre of fantasy – politically-corrected fairy-tales for grown-ups.

As we stand at the end of an age, where then shall we look for reasonable and energizing expectations? What must we do? How then shall we live? This is a question that has reappeared in contemporary Turkey, as Atatürk's vision begins to run out of steam.

Islam?

As modernist certainties dissolve in the acids of cynical post-modern skepticism, many intelligent observers believe that Islam holds the key to the Turkish future. The Justice and Development Party (*Adalet ve Kalkinma Partisi* or AKP) currently in power in Turkey thinks so, and young men are beginning to sport beards, young ladies to wear head coverings in public. Islam teaches a billion or more people on earth today to live with eternity in mind. Yet will this still be the case a century from now? Or even sooner?

"You can't fight something with nothing," the American political slogan goes. Applied to the issue of rebuilding broken worlds, we might rephrase that as, "You can't fight a worldview with a navel view." Larry Poston, a professor at Nyack College, researched and compared Christian and Muslim conversion stories. The reasons most young people give for embracing a Christian conversion experience are well known: guilt, shame, fear, and the lure of having a relationship with a Personal Savior who will deliver them from all of the above. Most Christian conversions happen to children, tapering off dramatically after the age of 20. The fascinating part of Poston's research concerned the reasons why people converted to Islam. These were frequently older people, usually, like Cat Stevens (Yusuf Mohammed), people in their 30s. They were attracted to such things as the egalitarian nature of Islam, with its dearth of hierarchy, the simplicity and apparent reasonability of Islam, and by the fact that the Muslim tradition has something to say about everything. Islam is a complete and full-orbed structure of meaning and guidance (Poston, 1990, pp. 23-25).

Like Soviet Communism, however, Islamic ideology depends on several layers of firewall. Only a minority of Muslims can actually read the Qur'an in Arabic, and the *madrassas* stress rote oral memorization and recitation. Even those who read Arabic, or attempt to struggle through a translation in their native language, find themselves baffled by several features of this document. For example, the Qur'an is not arranged chronologically, but by the length of the chapters, from the longest to the shortest. Topics and the persons speaking change abruptly within chapters. Of the 114 chapters, 71 were "abrogated" to some extent by chronologically later revelations (Citizen Warrior, 2010). Some parts of the Qur'an and Hadith, like some parts of the Bible, simply look embarrassing in translation. Some cultural traditions, that may or may not be a part of the core of Islam, can impede economic progress.

One influential Turkish Muslim scholar, M. Fethulla Gülen, advocates dialogue, cooperation, and understanding between faith and science, between Christian and Muslim. His foundation's periodical *The Fountain*, a slick international "magazine of critical, scientific and spiritual thought," published an article by a Christian writer about the rewards of building cross-cultural friendships (Smedley, 2008, pp. 34-37).

Perhaps Atatürk, to use the colorful American idiomatic expression, "threw out the baby with the bathwater." For him, there were no compromises possible with traditional Islam. A religion that provides so many of the earth's inhabitants with a sense of connection to the eternal order had only a small, controlled place in his new world order. For example, he took issue with the traditional Islamic model of the patriarchal family, with results that are still playing out.

Atatürk asserted that his beloved nation could never know progress as long as it insisted on hobbling half of its adult population. Today, more than half of the physicians in Turkey are female. Turkish women were given the franchise years before many of their European sisters. Turkish women enjoy success in many high-prestige occupations, including engineering and academia. The Turkish Republic is respected as a civilized, cultured, and admirable nation. It can be asked if that would be the case, however, if the Kemalists had not created a "wall of separation" between mosque and state (Morin, 2004, p. 55).

Secular status quo?

The modern era owes much to the Peace of Westphalia, which subordinated church to state in the West, and provided the model of laicism embraced by Atatürk. Yet, what did Atatürk offer his people in lieu of the hope of eternal life? As our discussion of nationalism demonstrated, this powerful ideology emerged in the aftermath of the Protestant Reformation, and culminated in the massive mechanized fratricides of the blood-soaked 20th century. This inspired John Lennon to wistfully sing:

> Imagine there's no countries
> It isn't hard to do
> Nothing to kill or die for
> And no religion too (Lennon, 1971)

Yet during its day, secular, this-worldly nationalism gave people a sense of participation in something bigger than themselves, a reason to get out of bed in the morning, read the Pravda with their coffee, and go to work to build a better future. Of the Turkish scholars studied, Kodaman asserted that "(t)he Turkish national government and laicist order can absolutely never be changed. Otherwise, it is impossible to establish or restore governmental or social peace" (1998). Kasaba viewed with anxiety the mutually exclusive absolutisms of the three main players on the Turkish stage, and hoped that they would step back from the brink of confrontation (2000). Kabaklı suggested that the cult of Atatürk had gone too far, and toppled over the precipice into an idolatry that made objective and realistic thought impossible (1998). Özyürek suggested that the "good old days," the golden era irradiated by the elderly memories of youthful zest, were irretrievably gone – and no one was quite sure what to replace them with (Özyürek, 2006).

Some Turks will march in their millions in support of secularism, which is still identified in the Turkish mind with such things as science, reason, efficiency, and Atatürk. Statism, one of the "Six Arrows of Kemalism," asserts that government bureaucrats can best direct national life in a wide panoply of areas, including banking, education, and heavy industry (Sansal, 2010). After all, if one's relation to the eternal order is subordinate to political dictates, can any other area of life be withheld from political oversight and regulation?

However, as civil governments become larger, they become less efficient and more intrusive. Eventually, the general public is more inclined to swear at the genius of Caesar, rather than by the genius of Caesar. There are limits to the messianic claims of the political order, and of its ruling elite. In his philippic poem *The Gods of the Copybook Headings,* Rudyard Kipling summed up the iron law of fiscal reality that is eventually encountered by state-centered social orders:

> In the Carboniferous Epoch
> we were promised abundance for all,
>
> By robbing selected Peter
> to pay for collective Paul;
>
> But, though we had plenty of money,
> there was nothing our money could buy,
>
> And the Gods of the Copybook Headings said:
> "If you don't work you die" (Kipling, 2010)

When escalating public debt is monetized, overheating printing presses penalize the provident and impoverish everyone. As the Weimer Republic learned, there are limits to how practical it is to rely upon hyperinflation to solve the problem of national bankruptcy. But what are the alternatives?

When the defining, overarching structures of life implode, what then should we do? Panic? Look for scapegoats? Start another war? These are questions that thoughtful people everywhere, including America, are also pondering. We would be wise, perhaps, to learn from a 5th-century African Christian, a 20th-century secularized Muslim Turk, and an

Armenian Calvinist, that panic and despair are not the only options when one's world comes to an end.

Contrasts

A thoughtful observer will learn from Atatürk's central failure as well as from his successes. Both Augustine and Atatürk faced an untenable situation, an end of age, end of empire crisis. Each man stepped into a massive demoralization, a psychological Chernobyl, when nothing made sense any more. And each man provided a reinterpretation of their world that gave their audiences hope, direction, and motivation.

In their most comprehensive written artifacts, Augustine and Atatürk gave approximately equal emphasis to the five major points that convincing world re-imagers must deal with. Both were able to lead their people past the immediate crisis, and into a new normal, a new reality, a new conception of what society could be like.

Yet, a few generations later, Atatürk's legacy is beginning to look unsteady, beginning to waver. By contrast, the power of Augustine's vision still, to this day, engrosses people seeking answers to the public challenges of life. The Protestant Reformers reached back behind Aquinas to take Augustine to their bosom. A continuous string of later sages and scholars credit the African bishop with framing the terms of their worldviews. These included Martin Luther, John Calvin, Jonathan Edwards, the father and son scholars Charles and A.A. Hodges, Abraham Kuyper, Rousas John Rushdoony, and other thinkers who recommend real-world applications of the Christian message.

What made the difference? As our quantitative comparison of *Nutuk* and *City* demonstrated, the points wherein these two writers differed were as striking as the points wherein they agreed. In art, the "vanishing point" is the part of the picture that governs the linear components, that place on the distant horizon where parallel lines converge. Although unseen, the vanishing point structures and dominates the entire picture. When we examined the prominent words that Augustine and Atatürk did not share, it became obvious, in every particular, that these two leaders targeted different destinations.

In the first area, Atatürk's *transcendence* was of a this-worldly variety, with a focus on national identity, challenges to that identity, and the roles of the official players in the drama. Augustine placed his emphasis upon the eternal order, and the relationship between individual people and their Creator. Atatürk's *hierarchy* was political, and defined fate, idea, and salvation as aspects of national existence. Augustine's hierarchy, again, pointed to God, to people, and to the words that defined their interrelationships. When it came to *ethics*, Atatürk thought primarily in terms of what was good for the Turkish nation and bad for the enemies of the Turkish nation. Augustine thought in terms of people living righteously or sinfully under the eye of God. What *oath* do people swear by? What ultimate force do they appeal to as a guarantor of their pledges? For Atatürk, the political order was paramount. For Augustine, God and Christ were appealed to in the name of the good and the worthy. Finally, Atatürk viewed a secure Turkish nation as the ultimate good he could bequeath to his people, and to the world. Augustine did not anticipate ultimate security in this world, but could offer his people a hope beyond this world.

An aphorism holds that "he who marries the spirit of the age is soon a widower." Kemal Atatürk, with his conviction that he was on the side of progress, on the side of the future, had embraced a vision of transcendent reality that leading thinkers around the world, and the general public, had come to take for granted. Yet, his transcendent Ultimate Concern only had reference to the present, material, measurable world. Augustine tapped into a vision of an order beyond time that nonetheless progressively revealed itself within time. Ultimately, man does not live by bread alone. A full life requires more than a full stomach.

Despite his ultimate lack of an ultimately transcendent frame of reference, Atatürk was able to achieve victories and progress that the traditional religious orders found beyond their grasp. Although his transcendence was flawed, Atatürk instinctively paid attention to the other components of a viable vision statement.

Unless religious people today also address issues of corporate structure, objective ethics, public identity, and the transmission of their values to future generations, they will suffer the fate of the losers in Atatürk's culture wars. A transcendent "navel view," a personal mystical piety, no matter how intense, will never suffice as a substitute for a full-orbed world view. If people are unable to provide their offspring with explanations for life that are at least as big and comprehensive as all of life, their more thoughtful children will jump ship and join forces with ideologies that do seem to offer answers.

Afterword

Why Nutuk?

In an effort to communicate the value of *Nutuk*, I have oversimplified the issues it addresses, and chosen words that underline the passionate significance this document has for those to whom it was addressed. I have made an effort to foreground my own prejudices, as an American Christian, and to represent fairly the history-changing power of this document to the Turkish Muslim, who continues to wrestle with a potent, but ambivalent, legacy.

I have also applied a few accessible software tools to the task of seeking out additional insights. This dissertation contains a description of the reasoning that went into the selection and use of Yoshikoder. It also describes the process followed for preparing the source data, running the program, and analyzing the output. Other scholars are invited to use the data dictionary I developed, and to apply it to other documents. The technique of comparing two similar documents to one or more subtly different documents was quite helpful for this project.

I believe this study will be of value to scholars investigating *Nutuk* and similar game-changing documents. Atatürk obviously did some things right. He answered the big questions in a plausible way, with a credibility that shaped the lives of tens of millions for the best part of a century. The "five-point covenant" model seems to fit both Nutuk and City, and to highlight the essential components of these two world-changing documents.

Readers and leaders, will, I trust, take away from this research a few fresh insights about the similar themes that two world-changers, from totally different worlds, incorporated into their rhetoric in order to persuasively offer hope in times of chaos.

Autobiographical postscript

> "The end of an age is always a time of turmoil, war, economic catastrophe, cynicism, lawlessness and distress. But it is also an era of heightened challenge and creativity, of issues, and their world-wide scope. Never has an era faced a more demanding and exciting crisis. This then, above all else, is the great and glorious era to live in, a time of opportunity, one requiring fresh and vigorous thinking, indeed, a glorious time to be alive." (Rushdoony, 113-114)

As a culture runs out of gas and begins to implode, do you go back? Or forward?

Essad Bey (Lev Nussimbaum) was a Jewish lad from central Asia who wrote prolifically in German, and lived through one catastrophe after another. As a young man who was nostalgic for the multi-ethnic Azerbaijan of his childhood, he converted to Islam, reasoning that the Ottoman Empire's umbrella had made the zesty, peaceful diversity possible. (Reiss, 2005)

One of the most poignant works of historical scholarship I ever read had the memorable title *Nostalgia for the Modern: State Secularism and Everyday Politics in Turkey*. Turkish scholar Esra Özürek interviewed the aging "children of the revolution" who remembered their own youth as a time of energy, vision, zest, and limitless new possibilities. Kemal Atatürk completely remade Turkish society in the decades following 1924, and new worlds of opportunity opened up for the proud citizens of a new nation. (Özürek, 2006)

A rather tedious novel, but one worth reading if your interests lie in that direction, is Umberto Eco's *The Name of the Rose*. As the narrator details, in detail, the various signs of social and cultural disruption, including a plethora of now-forgotten apocalyptic cults, the reader keeps thinking about the two things the monk/scribe narrating the tale could not foresee: the Reformation, and the printing press.

How does one resolve the claims of competing cultures? Which "story" does he embrace as his own heritage? How do you pick the winner?

Carl Smedley was town marshal of Mt. Dora, Florida, a century ago at the end of the open range era. Cowboys who did not like the new ways occasionally suffered beatings if caught with pliers in their saddlebags – they had a habit of making gates as they pleased in the barbwire fences, you see. On the other hand, Grandpap explained, "if you ever had to pull a cactus thorn out of your horse's hoof with your teeth, you'd know why pliers were important!" This Methodist cowboy met a Catholic governess who was on vacation with the family she served. Smitten, he drove a buckboard a thousand miles from central Florida to western Pennsylvania, converted to Catholicism, married a woman who died a half-mile from where she was born, and had lots of kids. He traded in the clean-air wide-open spaces for spectacular sunsets and a job in a steel mill, smoked a pack a day, and died of cancer at the age of 86.

The urban northern Catholic milieu is one component of my cultural identity. My mother's folks were part of the same story, since the Eastern Rite (Ukrainian) Catholic Church participated in the great achievement of integrating the tide of immigrants from southern and eastern Europe into the American mainstream a century ago.

As Catholics, we held other faiths in disdain – not a recipe for making friends, when we moved to a rural, southern,

Protestant area! At this point I began attending public schools, was steeped in the religion of Americanism, and found a way to navigate life in terms of that faith through the Boy Scouts of America. Like Freemasonry, the BSA preached the value of religious commitment, but refrained from picking the winner, since we were all part of a larger community that transcended sectarian differences.

Meanwhile, in the background, the Vietnam War quietly escalated.

Issues I perceived as irresolvable in the Catholic perspective (such as puberty and Darwinism) made the New Age perspective look attractive for a while. Why not dance with an evolving deity inside an evolving universe, for life after life? However, the studied rootlessness of this westernized Hinduism made a stable life, or personality, impossible. The harder I sought to find "the light within," the weirder I became.[6] Some world views work, others – don't.

During a disastrous first year in college, a few evangelical Christians spent hours over the course of months in friendly

---

[6] Of all conceivable forms of enlightenment the worst is what these people call the Inner Light. Of all horrible religions the most horrible is the worship of the god within. Any one who knows any body knows how it would work; any one who knows any one from the Higher Thought Centre knows how it does work. That Jones shall worship the god within him turns out ultimately to mean that Jones shall worship Jones. Let Jones worship the sun or moon, anything rather than the Inner Light; let Jones worship cats or crocodiles, if he can find any in his street, but not the god within. Christianity came into the world firstly in order to assert with violence that a man had not only to look inwards, but to look outwards, to behold with astonishment and enthusiasm a divine company and a divine captain. The only fun of being a Christian was that a man was not left alone with the Inner Light, but definitely recognized an outer light, fair as the sun, clear as the moon, terrible as an army with banners. *Orthodoxy*. G. K. Chesterton. http://www.gutenberg.org/cache/epub/130/pg130.html

confrontation. I faced the very real possibility that maybe they were right. The Son of Man might indeed be "the only game in town." If so, though, I would need to accept his terms, rather than try to negotiate my own. My conversion happened after a last-ditch attempt at flight, a frantic 200-mile bicycle ride. I now had a story, and started looking for a people who shared it. Amazingly enough, several of my drinking buddies from college had undergone the same experience. It was at this point that the conundrum of *Christ and Culture* (Niebuhr, 1951) became apparent. During an amazing moment, the "counterculture" suddenly wanted to hear about *The Man from Galilee*. (Ocean, 1971) Revival broke out, creating its own norms and forms and mores. We, the Jesus Freaks, had The REAL Thing, an intense and all-consuming religious experience. They, the "church Christians," had their traditions, their costumes, their rote routines, their tidy commercial charismata, and a structure that could chug along on its own just fine, thank you, with or without God.

Then, the Vietnam War ended, the counterculture predicated thereon faded into the nihilistic silliness of the disco era, and the apocalyptic brand of Christianity predicated on the counterculture was *Left Behind*. Our world ended. The world didn't. We were baffled.

For a while, I adopted the history of the Methodists as my own, attracted by John Wesley's achievement in transforming England for the better. I earned a Methodist license to preach, married a Methodist girl, and acquired a BA from a Methodist college. Cognitive dissonance set in again when I finally opened my eyes to the unpleasant fact that the agents of a different faith had long since hijacked the leadership and resources of the United Methodist Church. (Machen, 2007)

In the early 1980's, I came to grips with the position I hold today, an uneasy balancing act between the charismatic and

Calvinist strands of the Christian faith. I was influenced by the warmth of a Presbyterian pastor's preaching, and by the light shed on a number of issues by Presbyterian writers. A coterie of Reformed (that's what Calvinists call themselves) writers and thinkers are making systematic attempts to apply their faith to all of life, not just the "religious" part. I think it's a movement with a future, since it cherishes its deep roots in the past. We tend to be "bookish" folks with prehensile feet, the better to stand on the shoulders of giants, my dear! We can build upon the achievements of those who have gone before us, Catholic, Orthodox, and Protestant, to develop our understanding in terms of "the faith once handed to the saints," while vigorously and cheerfully contending with foes inside and outside the camp.

Rock-paper-scissors-lizard-Spock

Henry Van Til referred to culture as "religion externalized." (Van Til, p. 186, 2001) Another writer, Gary North, suggests that any culture needs to answer the following questions about ultimate reality:

1. What does a society believe about God?

2. What does a society believe about man?

3. What does a society believe about law?

4. What does a society believe about time? (North, p. 6, 1994)

When they can no longer offer convincing answers to these questions societies, like people, run out of gas. The 60's era counterculture embodied the suspicion that our leaders had misled us, and had something other than our good in mind as they kept a no-win war simmering as a back-burner money machine. Acts of "raw judicial activism" imposed unpopular, and even evil, mandates upon the public from leaders who had ceased to represent the citizen's best interests. The US Mint went into the counterfeiting business in order to fund the Vietnam War without (visibly) raising taxes, by debauching the coinage. More recently, the World Wide Web has permitted previously suppressed viewpoints to see the light of day, despite horrified admonitions to "ignore the little man behind the curtain."[7] When rulers and ruled, leaders and led, feel alienated from each other, change is afoot.

If the perceived power gap is too great, a surly discontent that endures, while despising, the status quo can rumble at a low boil of cynical resignation. Many Turkish proverbs reflect this attitude towards power: *Eski hamam, eski tas* (Same old bathhouse, same old washing bowl). *It ürür, kervan yürür* (The dogs bark, the caravan moves on). Sooner or later, though, a tipping point is reached, often catalyzed by something totally unexpected.[8]

The Soviet Union fell almost overnight when bootleg copies of *The Gulag Archipelago* circulated around the Soviet

---

[7] I don't need to cite *The Wizard of Oz*, since everyone's already seen it, probably many times! Parenthetically, the underlying theme is fiscal policy, especially that promoted by William Jennings Bryan, the "Lion of the Prairie." Dorothy encounters the gold standard (yellow brick road), the paper standard (Emerald City) and the bimetallic standard (silver slippers) that finally takes her home.

[8] Some fortuitous coincidence will render publicly obvious the structural contradictions between stated purposes and effective results in our major institutions. People will suddenly find obvious what is now evident to only a few . . . Like other widely shared insights, this one will have the potential of turning public imagination inside out. Large institutions can quite suddenly lose their respectability, their legitimacy, and their reputation for serving the public good. It happened to the Roman Church in the Reformation, to royalty in the Revolution. The unthinkable became obvious overnight: that people could and would behead their rulers. (Illich, p. 111, 1970)

managerial class, and the *nomenclatura* realized that they were wrong about the color of their hats. They were not heroic social engineers creating a new earthly paradise, but the architects of hells on earth. As anyone who lived through and studied the era can tell you, Communism was, for a while, a living faith that inspired millions of people.[9] Then, it wasn't. A conversation with an English teacher during a Dnieper River boat cruise broke my heart. She grew up seeing herself as part of the grand adventure, Ukrainians and Russians as Slavic brothers building a modern, scientific, utopia so wise, fair, and just that the whole world would envy it. Then, *glasnost* opened the records, and she learned that the Slavic brotherhood was more like that of Cain and Abel. The guards at the borders had their guns pointing in, to keep desperate comrades from escaping, rather than out, to fend off the eager aspirants to the collectivist dream. "I have a 14-year old son," she said, "And I'm glad that you are here to talk to us about God. I hope he will come to believe in God, because it's important to have something to believe in. I'm not ready to believe in anything, yet."

People of my generation grew up under the shadow of The Bomb. Walter Miller launched the "atom doom" franchise of science fiction with his novel *A Canticle for Leibowitz*, (Miller, 1960) written in penance for his role in destroying Monte Casino, the oldest monastery in Europe. Then, one day, the threat was gone. Soviet Communism lost its credibility, and lively missionaries planted churches in the former Soviet bloc. The largest congregation in Europe at the moment is a Pentecostal church in Kiev, founded by an African missionary. Russian school children soak up the Bible and Orthodox Christianity in their public schools.

---

[9] *Witness* by Whitaker Chambers is one of the great autobiographies of the 20th century. See also *Dedication and Leadership* by Douglas Hyde.

As he lay dying on the battlefield, Julian the Apostate hurled a handful of his own blood at the sky and said, "Thou hast conquered, O Galilean." In the cosmic game of Rock-paper-scissors-lizard-Spock,[10] Marxism declared war upon God and those who believed in God. Today, nearly 100 million Chinese Christians make their political masters a little bit nervous, since they pledge allegiance to a power that transcends "the barrel of the gun."

Nationalism is still a power. Since the Peace of Westphalia, the nation-state gave people something bigger than themselves to belong to, fight for, die for. The daily paper replaced the breviary, and agents of the State[11], ("God walking through history," if we believe Hegel!) replaced the parish priest. In lieu of a liturgical language, people added a semi-artificial national language to their local patois. A major theme of my dissertation was how secular nationalism trumped traditional Islam as the Ottoman Empire collapsed. Yet, "man does not live by bread alone," and it takes more than a full stomach to make a full life. The deity of nationalism is the nation itself, rather than any transcendent explanation for the nation. "Is that all there is?"

Islam is still a power to reckon with, since Muslims take very seriously the two things derided by America's Hollywood culture, the public face we present to the world: faith and family. Nearly a billion of our neighbors live dangerous, but non-boring lives, under the stern eye of Allah, convinced that a day of reckoning awaits on the other side of death. On the other hand, Islam depends upon a whole series of firewalls to maintain its hold on the imagination – and the Internet is poking holes through those firewalls.

---

[10] http://www.samkass.com/theories/RPSSL.html

[11] Government school teachers, e.g.

One of my heroes is the African Christian, probably "a man of color," whose thinking and writing defined the structure and self-concept of Europe for a thousand years. Like Atatürk, Augustine looked at a collapsing empire and said, "You know, we can do better."

Bottom line: I suspect we are watching the slow-motion collapse of the American faith in American leaders. Luke, companion of Paul, physician, historian, master stylist, and compassionate observer, postmortemed a nation whose leaders failed to grasp the significance of their day. The Sadducees, a secular elite who viewed politics as the only ultimate reality, and their entertainment / media franchises (the Pharisees and Scribes) joined forces to suppress the truth, caring more to feather their own nests than for their nation's salvation. The excellent movie *The City of Ember* imaginatively portrays the same tendency.

We are also watching the unsteady but purposeful first steps of a new Christian culture growing up under the radar. Millions of American families, Catholic and Protestant, politely decline to render unto Caesar that which they assert belongs to God – the children entrusted to their care. Stay tuned – these are exciting days to live in. As scholars of intercultural concepts, we must, I believe, examine our own presuppositions, and ponder the characteristics of a culture worthy to quietly, peacefully, and graciously replace what we have. Because the handwriting is on the wall. The United States of America have been weighed in the balances, and found wanting. No nation can declare war upon its own past and its own future, and endure in its present form.

But, there is a future and a hope. (Jer. 29:11) Our best days are ahead of us. As R. J. Rushdoony said in one of his pithy aphorisms, "Leave it to fools to wonder and imagine about the earth's last days. Serve God with joy and thanksgiving in these young days of His new creation."

References

Aaronsohn, A. (1916). *With the Turks in Palestine*. Retrieved from http://www.gutenberg.org/files/10338/10338-h/10338-h.htm

Abuladze, T. (Writer/Director). (1986). *Repentance* [Motion picture]. Russia: Image Entertainment.

Adak, H. (2003). National myths and self-na(rra)tions: Mustafa Kemal's Nutuk and Halide Edib's Memoirs and the Turkish ordeal. *The South Atlantic Quarterly*, 102.2/3, 509-527.

AECMA. (1989). *AECMA Simplified English*. Paris: Association Europeenne des Constructeurs de Materiel Aerospatial.

Ames, E. (1968). *Who Will Answer?* Retrieved December 13, 2010 from http://www.actionext.com/names_e/ed_ames_lyrics/who_will_answer.html

Anatolian Storms. (2008). *"With Henna In Their Palms" – Reflections Upon The Sacred, Sacrificial Sense Of Military Service*. Retrieved January 9, 2009 from http://anatolianstorm.blogspot.com/2008/02/with-henna-in-their-palms.html#links

Aristotle. (1912). *A Treatise On Government*. (William Ellis, Trans.). Retrieved from http://www.gutenberg.org/files/6762/6762-h/6762-h.htm (Original work published 1495).

Asimov, I. (2004). *The Foundation Trilogy*. New York: Science Fiction Book Club; Book Club edition.

Atatürk, M. (1985). *A Speech Delivered By Ghazi Mustapha Kemal Atatürk In October 1927: Nutuk*. (M. Kemal, Trans.). İstanbul: Üçdal Publishing Company. (Original work published 1927).

Atatürk, M. (1997). *Ghazi M. Kemal Atatürk Söylev: Cilt I-Ii. Nutuk* [Ghazi M. Kemal Atatürk's Lecture: Volumes I-II of Nutuk]. (H. Velidedeoğlu, Trans.). İstanbul: Yeni Gün Haber Ajansı. (Original work published 1927).

Atatürk, M. (2006). *Nutuk*. Retrieved March 3, 2006 from http://www.interaktifokul.com/english/Nutuk/Nutuk.asp

Atatürk, M. (2010). *Atatürk Says*. Retrieved March 4, 2010 from http://okulweb.meb.gov.tr/34/12/325300/ataturk_says.htm

Augustine, A. (1961). *The Confessions Of Saint Augustine*. New York: Collier Press.

Banfield, E. (1970). *The Unheavenly City: The Nature And Future Of Our Urban Crisis*. New York: Little, Brown.

Barnhart, S. (2004). *Bavaria's Last Form Of Self-Governing*. Retrieved November 2, 2005 from http://www.lewrockwell.com/barnhart/barnhart19.html

Baum, L. (1979). *The Wizard Of Oz*. New York: Ballentine Books.

Berger, P. & Luckmann, T. (1967). *The Social Construction Of Reality: A Treatise In The Sociology Of Knowledge*. Garden City, NY: Anchor Books.

Bhabha, H. (1990). *Nation And Narration*. London and New York. Routledge.

Bonaparte, N. (2009). *Napoleon Bonaparte Quotes*. Retrieved August 21, 2009 from http://thinkexist.com/quotation/history_is_a_set_of_lies_agr eed_upon/216931.html

Brown, D. (1981). *Bury My Heart At Wounded Knee*. New York: Washington Square Press.

Bujold, L. (1999). *Cordelia's Honor*. New York: Baen Books.

Burke, K. (2003). *On Human Nature: A Gathering While Everything Flows, 1967-1984*. Berkeley: University of California Press.

Bushman , R. (1980). *From Puritan To Yankee: Character And The Social Order In Connecticut, 1690-1765*. Cambridge, MA: Harvard University Press.

Butler, S. (2010) *War Is A Racket*. Retrieved November 16, 2010 from http://www.lexrex.com/enlightened/articles/warisaracket.htm

Calvin, J. (2010) *The Institutes Of The Christian Religion*. Retrieved from http://www.iclnet.org/pub/resources/text/ipb-e/epl-09/cvin4-22.txt

Simpson, D. (Ed.). (1960). *Cassell's New Latin Dictionary*. New York: Funk & Wagnalls.

Chambers, W. 1987. *Witness*. Regnery Publishing.

Citizen Warrior (pseud.). (2010). *The Qur'an Is Written In Code*. Retrieved September 16, 2010 from http://www.citizenwarrior.com/2010/08/quran-is-written-in-code.html

Collodi, C. (Carlo Lorenzini). (1983). *The Adventures Of Pinocchio*. (Nicolas Perella, Trans.). Berkeley and Los Angeles: University of California Press.

Davison, A. (1998). *Secularism And Revivalism In Turkey: A Hermeneutic Reconsideration*. New Haven and London: Yale University Press.

Delaney, C. (1995). Father state, motherland, and the birth of Modern Turkey. In S. Yanagisako & C. Delaney (Eds.), *Naturalizing Power: Essays In Feminist Cultural Analysis* (pp. 177-199). New York: Routledge.

DeMar, G. (1987). *Ruler Of The Nations: Biblical Principles For Government*. Ft. Worth, TX: Dominion Press.

Downing, T. & Fox, D. (1995). *HTML Web Publisher's Construction Kit*. Corte Madera, CA: The Waite Group.

Dwyer, J. (2006). *Hegel And The Cunning Of History*. Retrieved August 21, 2009 from http://opencopy.org/lectures/intellectual-history/05-hegel-and-the-cunning-of-history/

Eco, U. (1980, 1983). *The Name Of The Rose*. (William Weaver, Trans.). New York: Warner Books, Inc.

Eusebius. (1990). *The History Of The Church: From Christ To Constantine*. (Andrew Louth, Trans.). New York: Penguin Classics.

Finkel, C. (2005). *Osman's Dream: The Story Of The Ottoman Empire 1300 - 1923*. New York: Basic Books.

Fortna, B. (2002). *Imperial Classroom: Islam, The State, And Education In The Late Ottoman Empire*. New York: Oxford University Press.

Frank, D. (1986). *Less Than Conquerors: How Evangelicals Entered The Twentieth Century*. Grand Rapids, MI: William B. Eerdmans Publishing Company.

Gellert, M. (2001). *The Fate Of America: An Inquiry Into National Character*. Dulles, VA: Brassey's, Inc.

Gibbon, E. (1898). *History Of The Decline And Fall Of The Roman Empire*. New York: Harper Brothers.

"Edward Gibbon." (n.d.). In Wikiquote. Retrieved February 24, 2010 from http://en.wikiquote.org/wiki/Edward_Gibbon

Gökkuşağı Türkçe Öğretim Seti. (2004). İstanbul. Zambak Basım Yayın Eğitim ve Trizm İşletmetleri Sanayi Ticaret.

Gold, D. (2003). *Hatred's Kingdom: How Saudi Arabia Supports The New Global Terrorism*. Washington, D.C.: Regnery Publishers, Inc.

Göle, N. (1994). Toward an autonomization of politics and civil society in Turkey. In A. Evin & M. Heper (Eds.), *Politics In The Third Turkish Republic*. Boulder: Westview Press.

Gülalp, H. (2005). Enlightenment by fiat: Secularization and democracy in Turkey. *Middle Eastern Studies*, 41 (3), 351-372.

Güler, Ö. (2007). Unpublished scholarly paper.

Hall, R. (2000). *The Balkan Wars 1912-1913*. New York: Routledge.

Harcourt-Rivington, S. (2009). *It Started With Plato*. Mises Daily. Retrieved November 9, 2010 from http://mises.org/daily/3620

Hegel, G. (2008). *Philosophy Of Right.* (S. Dyde, Trans.). New York: Cosimo Inc.

Hemingway, E. (1936). *The Snows Of Kilimanjaro.* Retrieved August 19, 2009 from http://www.geocities.com/andtherewaswater/Archive/TheSnowsOfKilimanjaro.htm

Hesse, H. (1968). *Beneath The Wheel.* (M. Roloff, Trans.). New York: Picador.

Hofstadter, D. (1979). *Gödel, Escher, Bach: An Eternal Golden Braid.* New York: Basic Books.

Hugo, V. (1889). *Les Miserables.* (C. Williams, Trans.). New York: Carleton.

Huizinga, J. (1954). *The Waning Of The Middle Ages.* New York: Doubleday Anchor.

Huntington, S. (1993, Summer). The clash of civilizations. *Foreign Affairs*, 72 (3), 42.

Hyde, D. (1966). *Dedication And Leadership: Learning From The Communists.* Notre Dame, IN: University of Notre Dame Press.

Illich, Ivan. 1970. *Tools for Conviviality.* New York, NY: Harper & Row, Publishers

Internet Movie Data Base (IMDB). (2009). *Memorable Quotes From The Third Man.* Retrieved August 19, 2009 from http://www.imdb.com/title/tt0041959/quotes

Jerome. (n.d.). *The Fall Of Rome.* Retrieved February 22, 2010 from http://www.eyewitnesstohistory.com/fallofrome.htm

Johnson, P. (1988). *A Shopkeeper's Millennium: Society And Revivals In Rochester, New York, 1815-1837.* New York: Hill and Wang.

Johnston, Mark D. (1987). *The Spiritual Logic Of Ramon Llull.* Oxford: Clarendon Press. Retrieved March 6, 2010 from

http://www-mat.upc.es/grup_de_grafs/logo/llull_bio.htm

Judt, T. (1992). *Past Imperfect: French Intellectuals, 1944-1956*. Berkeley and Los Angeles: University of California Press.

Kabaklı, A. (1998). Atatürk ve Atatürkçüler. *Yeni Turkiye* 98 (23-24).

Kasaba, R. (2000). Kemalist certainties and modern ambiguities. In S. Bozdogan & R. Kasaba (Eds.), *Rethinking Modernity And National Identity In Turkey*. Seattle: University of Washington Press.

Kenan, Gil (Director), Thompson, Caroline (screenplay), Duprau, Jeanne (book). 2008. *City of Ember*. http://www.imdb.com/title/tt0970411/

Kern, K. (1975). The owner-built home. New York: Scribner.

Keyman, E. (1997, Spring). *Kemalizm, Modernite, Gelenek: Türkiye'de "Demokratik Açılım" Olasığı*. (Kemalism, modernity, and tradition). Toplum ve Bilim 72.

Kinross, P. (1965). *Atatürk: A Biography Of Mustafa Kemal, Father Of Modern Turkey*. New York: William Morrow and Company.

Kipling, R. (2010). *The Gods Of The Copybook Headings*. Retrieved November 16, 2010 from http://www.kipling.org.uk/poems_copybook.htm

Kodaman, B. (1998). *Atatük'un Milli Birlik Ve Milli Devlet Anlayışı* (Atatürk's insights into national unity and national government). (T. Smedley, Trans.) Yeni Turkiye 98 (23-24).

Lacey, G. (2005, September). The impending collapse of Arab civilization. In *Naval Institute: Proceedings*. Retrieved August 3, 2009 from http://www.military.com/NewContent/0,13190,NI_0905_Arab-P1,00.html

Lamont, I. (2008). *Making A Case For Quantitative Research In The Study Of Modern Chinese History: The New China News Agency And Chinese Policy Views Of Vietnam, 1977☐ 1993*. (Master's thesis). Harvard University: Cambridge, MA.

Lancaster, D. (1978). *The Incredible Secret Money Machine*. Indianapolis, IN: Howard W. Sams.

Lennon, J. (1971). *Imagine*. Retrieved November 21, 2010 from http://www.oldielyrics.com/lyrics/john_lennon/imagine.html

Lewis, B. (1968). *The Emergence Of Modern Turkey*. New York: Oxford University Press.

Lewis, C. (1974). *The Abolition Of Man*. New York: Harper Collins.

Lewis, C. (2001). *The Screwtape Letters*. New York: Harper Collins.

Lewis, G. (1960). *Turkey*. New York: Frederick A. Praeger.

Lewis, G. (2002). *The Turkish Language Reform: A Catastrophic Success*. Retrieved June 5, 2007 from http://www.turkishlanguage.co.uk/jarring.htm

Llewellyn, R. (1997). *How Green Was My Valley*. Simon & Schuster: New York.

Machen, J. Gresham. 2007. *Christianity and Liberalism*. Downloaded 4/4/2014 from http://www.extremetheology.com/files/MachenLiberalism.pdf.

Manzoni, A. (1967). *I Promessi Sposi*. Milan, Italy: Editrice Lucchi.

May, R. (1969). *Love And Will*. New York: Dell Publishing Company, Inc.

Mears, E. (1924). *Modern Turkey: A Politico-Economic Interpretation, 1908-1923 Inclusive, With Selected Chapters By Representative Authorities*. New York: The Macmillan Company.

Merle, R. (1975). *Malevil*. New York: Warner Paperback Library.

Meyer, K. (2003, Winter). Let me hear my brother! *World Policy Journal*. Retrieved July 24, 2007 from http://findarticles.com/p/articles/mi_hb6669/is_4_20/ai_n29059103/pg_2/?tag=content;col1

Miller, Walter Mr. Jr., 1960. *A Canticle for Leibowitz*. J. B. Lippincott & Co. Philadelphia.

Mora, P. (Director). (1983). *The Return Of Captain Invincible* [Motion picture]. Australia: Seven Keys Production.

Neuendorf, K. (2004). *Computer Content Analysis*. Retrieved August 21, 2009 from http://academic.csuohio.edu/kneuendorf/content/cpuca/cca.htm

Niebuhr, H. Richard. 1951. *Christ and Culture*. Harper & Row, Publishers. New York.

Nietzsche, F. (1918). *The Antichrist*. (H.L. Menchen, Trans.). Retrieved August 21, 2009 from http://www.gutenberg.org/files/19322/19322-8.txt

North, G. (1996). *Crossed Fingers: How The Liberals Captured The Presbyterian Church*. Tyler, TX: Institute for Christian Economics.

North, Gary. *Unconditional Surrender, God's Program for Victory*. 4th ed. Tyler, Texas: Institute for Christian Economics, 1994. www.garynorth.com/freebooks/docs/214a_47e.htm .

Norwood, F. (1974). *The Story Of American Methodism*. Nashville, TN: Abingdon Press.

Ocean. 1971. *Put your hand in the hand of the man from Galilee*. Downloaded 4/4/2014 from https://www.youtube.com/watch?v=JI1DiddWCKs .

O'Meara, J. (1973). *An Augustine Reader*. Garden City, New York: Image Books.

Okrent, A. (2009). *In The Land Of Invented Languages: Esperanto Rock Stars, Klingon Poets, Loglan Lovers, And The Mad Dreamers Who Tried To Build A Perfect Language*. New York: Spiegel & Grau.

Orwell, G. (1977). *1984*. New York: New American Library.

Orwell, G. (1993). *Animal Farm*. New York: Alfred A. Knopf.

Özyürek, E. (2006). *Nostalgia For The Modern: State Secularism And Everyday Politics In Turkey*. Durham, NC and London, UK: Duke University Press.

Pamuk, O. (2002). *My name is red.* (Erdag Goknar, Trans.). New York: Vintage.

Pamuk, O. (2008). *Other colors: Essays and a story.* New York: Vintage.

Pardi, W. (1999). *XML in action.* Redmond, WA: Microsoft Press.

Paul, R. (1964). *The Lord Protector: Religion and politics in the life of Oliver Cromwell.* Grand Rapids, MI: William B. Eerdmans Publishing House.

Pei, M. (1965). *The story of language.* Philadelphia & New York: J. B. Lippincott Co.

Plato. (1998). *Republic.* (Robin Waterfield, Trans.). New York: Oxford University Press. (Original work published 360 B.C.E.).

Podles, L. (1999). *The Church impotent: The feminization of Christianity.* Dallas: Spence Publishing Company.

Poston, L. (1990, August). The adult gospel. *Christianity Today,* 23-25.

Rand, A. (1970). *The new left: The anti-industrial revolution.* New York: Signet.

Reed, C. (Writer). (1949). *The Third Man* [Motion picture]. London: London Film.

Reiss, T. (2006). *The Orientalist: Solving the mystery of a strange and dangerous life.* New York: Random House.

Reza, A. (2009). *How to win a cosmic war: God, globalization, and the end of the war on terror.* New York: Random House.

Roberts, P. (2009). *Obama's Speech.* Retrieved June 6, 2009 from http://www.lewrockwell.com/roberts/roberts268.html

Rushdoony, R. (1980). *Intellectual Schizophrenia: Culture, Crisis And Education.* Phillipsburg, NJ: Presbyterian and Reformed Publishing Company.

Saggs, H. (2000). *Babylonians (Peoples Of The Past).* Berkeley, Los Angeles, & London: University of California Press.

Sandars, N. (1972). *The Epic Of Gilgamesh: An English Version With An Introduction*. London: Penguin Books, Ltd.

Sansal, S. (2010). *Kemalism*. Retrieved November 16, 2010 from http://www.allaboutturkey.com/ata_prensip.htm

Sevier, A. (1922). *Islam And The Psychology Of The Musulman*. (A. Moss-Blundell, Trans.). London: Chapman Hall Ltd.

Seymour, J. (1978). *The Self-Sufficient Gardener*. Oxford: Oxford University Press.

Shaeffer, F. (1976). *How Should We Then Live?: The Rise And Decline Of Western Thought And Culture*. Wheaton, IL: Crossway Books.

Shaw, G. (1959). *Man And Superman: A Comedy And A Philosophy*. New York: Bantam Books.

Sibellius, J. (2010). Jean Sibelius quotes. Retrieved September 1, 2010 from http://thinkexist.com/quotes/jean_sibelius/

Smedley, T. (1992). *Social Maturity Of Home School Children: A Communication Approach*. Retrieved November 2, 2005 from http://www.tomsmedley.com/smedleys.htm .

Smedley, T. (2008, September/October). Turning the tables to build intercultural friendships. *The Fountain: A Magazine Of Critical, Scientific, And Spiritual Thought*, 34-37.

Solzhenitsyn, A. (1985). *The Gulag Archipelago 1918 - 1956*. New York: Harper and Row, Publishers, Inc.

Sowell, T. (1995). *The Vision Of The Anointed: Self-Congratulation As A Basis Of Social Policy*. New York: Basic Books

Spence, J. (1996). *God's Chinese Son: The Taiping Heavenly Kingdom Of Hong Xiuquan*. New York: W. W. Norton & Company, Inc.

Stanford Encyclopedia of Philosophy. *Karl Marx*. Retrieved October 26, 2010 from http://plato.stanford.edu/entries/marx/

Thomas, L. (1967). *With Laurence In Arabia*. New York: Doubleday.

Time Magazine. (2000). The most influential people of the 20th century. *Time Magazine*. Retrieved from http://www.time.com/time/time100/time100poll.html

Tipple, E. (1916). *Francis Asbury: The Prophet Of The Long Road.* New York: The Methodist Book Concern.

Sampson, P. (1999, January/February). *Repeating History*. Eclectica. Retrieved from http://www.eclectica.org/v3n1/sampson_history.html

Ucuzsatar, N. (2002). The dissolution of the Ottoman Empire and the foundation of modern Turkey under the leadership of Mustafa Kemal Atatürk [Electronic version]. *Journal Of İstanbul Kültür University*, 2, 55-68.

Van Til, Henry. 2001. *Calvinistic Concept of Culture, The*. Baker Academic.

Vint, D. (1999). *SGML At Work*. Upper Saddle River, NJ: Prentice Hall PTR.

Weaver, R. (1984). *Ideas Have Consequences*. Chicago: University of Chicago Press.

Weir, P. (Director). (1982). *The Year Of Living Dangerously* [Motion picture]. MGM.

Wheeler, T. (2006). *Mr. Lincoln's T-Mails: How Abraham Lincoln Used The Telegraph To Win The Civil War*. New York: Harper Collins Publishers.

Wilder, T. (2004). *The Bridge of San Luis Rey*. New York: Harper Collins.

Wills, G. (1999). Saint Augustine. New York: Viking.

Zambak, M. (2007). A river of flags in İstanbul in support of secular democracy. Retrieved July 2, 2007 from http://www.asianews.it/index.php?l=en&art=9133&geo=49&size=A

Appendix A: Data Dictionary

```xml
<?xml version="1.0" encoding="UTF-8"?>
<dictionary style="050805" patternengine="substring">
  <cnode name="Smedley dictionary 6" desc="Nutuk power words">

        <cnode name="" desc="1_Transcendence">
        <pnode name="accurately"/>
                <pnode name="certainty"/>
                <pnode name="confident"/>
                <pnode name="confirm"/>
                <pnode name="contradict"/>
                <pnode name="enlightened"/>
                <pnode name="evidently"/>
                <pnode name="fitting"/>
                <pnode name="lasting"/>
                <pnode name="permanent"/>
                <pnode name="persist"/>
                <pnode name="preservation"/>
                <pnode name="preserving"/>
                <pnode name="presumption"/>
                <pnode name="resisted"/>
                <pnode name="sides"/>
                <pnode name="soil"/>
                <pnode name="solid"/>
                <pnode name="treasure"/>
        </cnode>
        <cnode name="" desc="2_Community">
                <pnode name="acquainted"/>
                <pnode name="addressing"/>
                <pnode name="communities"/>
                <pnode name="contribute"/>
                <pnode name="customs"/>
                <pnode name="medical"/>
                <pnode name="native"/>
                <pnode name="patriarch"/>
                <pnode name="promising"/>
                <pnode name="rendering"/>
                <pnode name="therein"/>
                <pnode name="touched"/>
                <pnode name="treatment"/>
                <pnode name="withdrawn"/>
                <pnode name="yourselves"/>
        </cnode>
```

```
<cnode name="" desc="3_Ethics">
        <pnode name="absence"/>
        <pnode name="adapted"/>
        <pnode name="afforded"/>
        <pnode name="bloodshed"/>
        <pnode name="changing"/>
        <pnode name="complain"/>
        <pnode name="cruelties"/>
        <pnode name="cry"/>
        <pnode name="deceiving"/>
        <pnode name="dependent"/>
        <pnode name="exceed"/>
        <pnode name="excuse"/>
        <pnode name="increasing"/>
        <pnode name="inflict"/>
        <pnode name="lacking"/>
        <pnode name="method"/>
        <pnode name="murdered"/>
        <pnode name="obtaining"/>
        <pnode name="path"/>
        <pnode name="practice"/>
        <pnode name="prime"/>
        <pnode name="so-called"/>
        <pnode name="spend"/>
</cnode>
<cnode name="" desc="4_Judicial">
        <pnode name="convicted"/>
        <pnode name="deemed"/>
        <pnode name="differ"/>
        <pnode name="expresses"/>
        <pnode name="governing"/>
        <pnode name="popular"/>
        <pnode name="preference"/>
        <pnode name="prefers"/>
        <pnode name="punish"/>
        <pnode name="reminded"/>
        <pnode name="requisite"/>
        <pnode name="warned"/>
</cnode>
<cnode name="" desc="5_Time">
        <pnode name="accomplish"/>
        <pnode name="acquired"/>
        <pnode name="attainment"/>
        <pnode name="beforehand"/>
        <pnode name="closed"/>
```

```
                <pnode name="lastly"/>
                <pnode name="originally"/>
                <pnode name="recent"/>
                <pnode name="sooner"/>
                <pnode name="terminated"/>
                <pnode name="threw"/>
                <pnode name="thrown"/>
        </cnode>

    </cnode>
</dictionary>
```

Atatürk's *Büyük Nutuk* and Augustine's *City of God*

88494615R00125

Made in the USA
Lexington, KY
12 May 2018